Spelling Rules!

Janelle Ho and
Helen Pearson

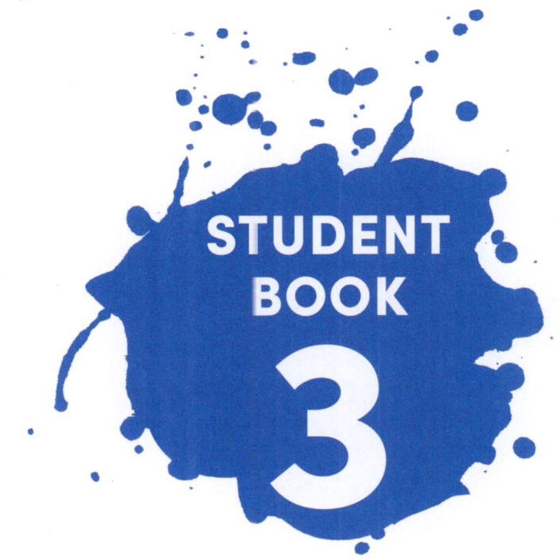

Australian Curriculum Edition

Name: ______________________________

Class: ______________________________

Contents

SLLURP

SLLURP summarises the spelling strategies that you can use to learn new words.

Say	Say the word carefully and slowly to yourself.
Listen	Listen to how each part of the word sounds in sequence.
Look	Look at the patterns of letters in the word and the shape of the word.
Understand	Understand rules, word meanings and word origins.
Remember	Remember all the similar words you can already spell and relate this knowledge to any new word.
Practise	Practise writing the word until it is firmly fixed in your long-term memory.

Spelling Fules! Student Book 3 (ISBN 9780655092698) © Janelle Ho, Helen Pearson

Scope and Sequence

Unit	SKILL FOCUS: Vowels	Consonants	Letter patterns	Morphology and etymology	Homophones/ Confusing words	Topic words	WORD LIST
1	a-e, i-e			-ed; irregular verbs and plurals	brake/break		brave, shade, brake, table, awake, aeroplane, while, beside, spite, alive, advise, promise
2	o-e, u-e			-ing, -y			close, alone, erode, suppose, approve, wardrobe, huge, pure, cube, refuse, accuse, conclude
3	oo, ee, ea, ai, oa				to/too/two, rowed/road/rode, great/grate		shook, blood, choose, soothe, bleed, breath, breathe, threat, explain, throat, poach, cockroach
4			ow, ou, oy ey, ay				know, growl, below, allow, touch, grouchy, pounce, mountain, royal, money, trolley, layer
5				words beginning with a-, al-, un-, dis-			across, always, about, around, almost, already, ahead, asleep, above, another, along, altogether
6	REVISION						
7		ch				compound words with ache	school, ache, echo, choir, character, chorus, chameleon, stomach, monarch, anchor, chef, machine
8				proper nouns, apostrophes of possession		Australian states and territories, and capitals	country, state, northern, western, south, capital, territory, Australia, New South Wales, Victoria, Tasmania, Queensland
9				-er, -est		Aboriginal Australian words	Mob, Elder, Auntie, Uncle, deadly, gammon, tucker, humpy, yakka, yidaki, boomerang, marngrook
10	ie, ei				peace/piece, cheap/cheep, steel/steal		grief, relief, fierce, niece, sieve, thieve, believe, friend, weird, receive, ceiling, foreign
11				un-, mis-, dis-			untidy, unlikely, mischief, misplace, misbehave, mistake, disagree, disgrace, disgusting, dishonest, disobey, discover
12	REVISION						
13				-ful, -less: changing y to i			helpful, awful, harmful, peaceful, colourful, grateful, beautiful, helpless, useless, careless, fearless, lifeless
14	au, aw						taut, haul, fault, pause, sauce, sausage, audio, flaw, thaw, drawer, sprawl, awesome
15		medial double consonants					gallop, collide, tunnel, channel, tennis, rubbish, common, lesson, borrow, quarrel, affect, effect
16		silent letters: kn, wr	le				apple, saddle, puddle, riddle, cuddle, bubble, bottle, kettle, little, juggle, giggle, wriggle
17						months of the year	January, February, March, April, May, June, July, August, September, October, November, December
18	REVISION						
19			igh, eigh, ough, augh	irregular past tense verbs			midnight, frighten, neighbour, rough, enough, though, through, thought, caught, taught, daughter, naughty
20		gh, ph		tele, phone, photo, auto, graph			laugh, toughen, graph, photograph, autograph, elephant, telephone, sphere, trophy, alphabet, phrase, physical
21		words ending in f, ff, fe, ffe		changing f to v; collective nouns			puff, cliff, staff, shelf, wolf, scarf, wharf, thief, knife, handkerchief, yourself, giraffe
22	words ending in o, oe, oo, a			irregular plurals	confusing words: there/their/they're		hero, piano, zero, radio, toe, canoe, kangaroo, taboo, sofa, drama, idea, era
23				-ness, -ion, -ship, -dom, -hood, -wards			kindness, happiness, revision, television, direction, friendship, kingdom, freedom, forwards, backwards, childhood, neighbourhood
24	REVISION						
25		silent letters: kn, wr, t, gn, h, s, b				non-English words	wrinkle, wrestle, knead, knowledge, gnaw, gnome, hour, honest, island, tongue, doubt, ghost
26		soft and hard c; sce, sci					carpet, cancel, once, lettuce, advice, cucumber, cylinder, because, decide, scent, science, scissors
27		soft and hard g			great/grate, grown/groan, guest/guessed		gather, guest, guide, together, germ, gentle, genius, giant, large, stage, gigantic, gypsy
28			dge				edge, hedge, badge, fridge, bridge, judge, nudge, trudge, smudge, dodge, fidget, gadget
29			qu		quit/quiet/quite		quiet, quite, queue, quarter, squirm, squeal, squawk, equal, request, require, squirrel, mosquito
30	REVISION						
31				uni-, bi-, tri-, kilo-, dec-, centi-, milli-		measurement	metre, kilometre, centimetre, millimetre, litre, gram, decade, uniform, bicycle, triangle, dozen, dollar
32			ex	in-			exit, extra, expert, experience, extreme, example, exact, excuse, excellent, exclaim, excite, exercise
33			ion	-ion			station, fiction, section, fraction, cushion, fashion, mission, expression, religion, million, champion, information
34					desert/dessert, course/coarse	non-English words	igloo, robot, yacht, iceberg, khaki, tsunami, kindergarten, kowtow, pizza, spaghetti, chocolate, restaurant
35	REVISION						

NOTE TO TEACHERS AND PARENTS

Spelling Rules!

Some students are natural spellers. But the vast majority of students need formal, systematic and sequential instruction about the way spelling works and the strategies they can use to become independent, confident spellers and spelling risk-takers.

The *Spelling Rules!* program is based on sound linguistic and pedagogical theory. It is informed by research into how students of different ages acquire and apply spelling skills, and how those skills move from the working to the long-term memory. The program closely follows the Australian English curriculum. *Australian Curriculum: English* references are provided in the Teacher Resource Books. The program consists of seven student books, fully supported by two Teacher Resource Books.

Each student book contains units of work, with each unit designed to be used over the course of a week. The content of each unit simultaneously develops new skills and reinforces skills from previous units. The introduction of new sounds and letter patterns is logically sequenced and takes into account both frequency of use and complexity. Where appropriate, topic words from other curriculum areas such as mathematics, science and social sciences are included. When spelling rules are introduced, only known sounds and letter patterns are used so that students focus on one skill at a time. Regular revision units enable teachers to assess student progress and reinforce key rules and patterns from previous units.

The *Spelling Rules!* program also incorporates elements of self-assessment. A simple reflection activity allows students to assess their own progress and provides you with a starting point for discussion.

Spelling knowledge

Learning to spell involves developing different kinds of spelling knowledge:

- **Kinaesthetic knowledge** – the physical feeling when saying different sounds and words, and when writing the shapes of letters and words
- **Phonological knowledge** – how a word sounds and the patterns of sounds in words
- **Visual knowledge** – how letters and words look and the visual patterns in words
- **Morphemic knowledge** – the meaning or function of words or parts of words
- **Etymological knowledge** – the origins and history of words and the effect this has on spelling patterns.

Icons used in Student Book 3

The following icons identify the main spelling strategy that students will use to complete an activity.

Say the word. (Kinaesthetic knowledge) These activities ask students to experience how sounds feel in the mouth and jaw. Changing the positions of the jaw, lips and tongue changes the sounds we make. Encourage students to pronounce the sounds and words accurately. If they mispronounce a sound or word, they may misrepresent it in writing.

Listen to the word. (Phonological knowledge) These activities focus on discriminating between different sounds and breaking up words into syllables or individual sound segments (phonemes).

Look at the word. (Visual knowledge) These activities help students to see how the sound is represented using combinations of letters, and to associate this visual pattern with what they are hearing. Students will develop the ability to know when a word does or does not 'look right'.

Understand the word. (Morphemic and etymological knowledge) These activities focus on word meanings, word families, prefixes and suffixes, spelling rules, word origins and so on, which help embed spelling in the long-term memory.

Practise writing the word. (Kinaesthetic knowledge) These activities develop students' awareness of the physical movement involved in writing the word. By practising writing the word a number of times and in different contexts, the spelling becomes embedded in the long-term memory.

This icon highlights useful spelling rules.

This icon tells students that a special clue or hint is provided for an activity. It may be a spelling, grammar or punctuation convention, or a definition of a useful term.

Encourages students to assess their progress across each unit.

Spelling Rules! Student Book 3 (ISBN 9780655092698) © Janelle Ho, Helen Pearson

Student Book 3

Units of work

Student Book 3 contains 35 weekly units of work. See the **Scope and Sequence chart** on page 3 for more information. Each revision unit gives students an opportunity to self-assess.

Word lists

In *Student Book 3*, each unit (except Revision) has a list of spelling words. The core words in the lists have been chosen to support the learning focus and strategies being taught in the unit.

Spelling lists enable a spelling element to be focused on, and provide sufficient examples to consolidate the teaching point. Topic words come from other curriculum areas, such as mathematics and social sciences. In addition, homophones and words that are easily confused with each other are explained and practised.

SLLURP

Each word list begins with a reminder for students to SLLURP. SLLURP summarises the strategies that will help spelling move from students' working memory to their long-term memory. These strategies are provided on page 2, for easy reference.

Unit at a glance

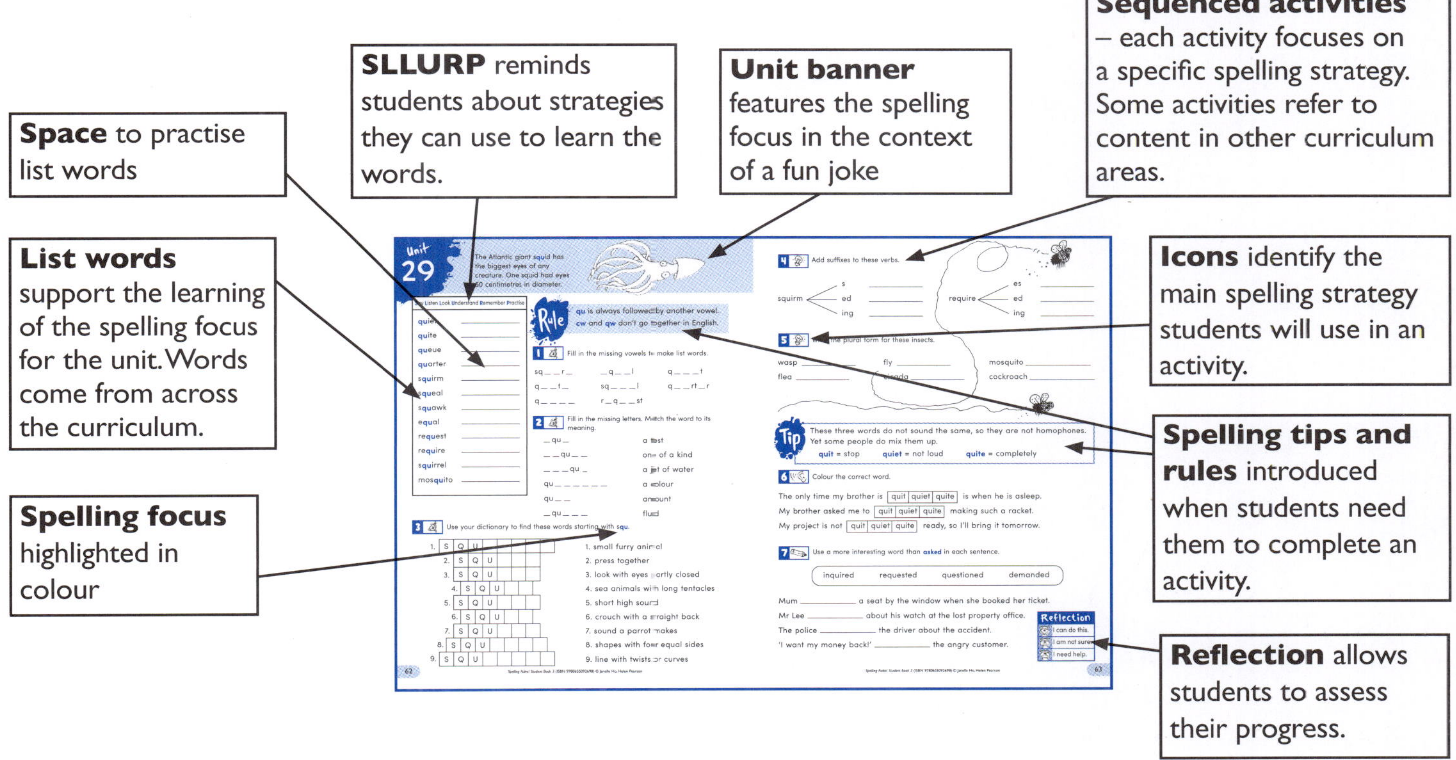

Spelling Rules! Teacher Resource Book 3–6

Full teacher support for *Student Book 3* is provided by *Spelling Rules! Teacher Resource Book 3–6*. Here you will find valuable background information about spelling development and spelling knowledge, along with practical resources, such as:

- teaching tips for every unit in *Student Book 3*
- extra word lists
- strategies for teaching spelling
- guidelines for assessment and diagnosis of errors
- activities to support struggling spellers
- worthwhile extension for more able spellers.

Unit 1

Tapeworms can live inside people. They can be up to 25 metres long – that's the length of two buses!

Say Listen Look Understand Remember Practise

brave ____________
shade ____________
brake ____________
table ____________
awake ____________
aeroplane ____________
while ____________
beside ____________
spite ____________
alive ____________
advise ____________
promise ____________

1 Find a list word that rhymes. Write another word that follows the **a-e** or **i-e** pattern.

gain ____________ ____________
lied ____________ ____________
label ____________ ____________
smile ____________ ____________
drive ____________ ____________
quite ____________ ____________
save ____________ ____________
stayed ____________ ____________

Write the two list words that have the same ending but do not rhyme.

____________ ____________

2 Write an **a-e** word to match each meaning.

f_ _ _ the front of your head
sh_ _ _ you don't do this if you want a beard
sn_ _ _ a reptile with no legs
br_ _ _ willing to face danger

3 Write an **i-e** word to match each meaning.

sl_ _ _ slip downwards
pr_ _ _ what something costs
m_ _ _ more than one mouse
in_ _ _ _ not outside

Spelling Rules! Student Book 3 (ISBN 9780655092698) © Janelle Ho, Helen Pearson

4 Colour the correct word.

Boil the eggs in a | pan | pane | of water, then cool them in a | tub | tube |.

Our | car | care | was parked for too long and we got a | fin | fine |.

Tomatoes turn red when they are | rip | ripe |.

Rule

For most verbs ending in **e**, you drop the **e** before adding **ed** to make the past tense. *live → lived* *bake → baked*

But be careful – some verbs do not follow this rule!

make → made *drive → drove* *wake → woke*

5 Complete each sentence by writing the verb in the past tense.

Jane ____________ her dog for messing up her homework.
blame

Mrs Smith ____________ us to read for 20 minutes each day.
advise

Sanjay ____________ on the wet leaves and hurt his foot.
slide

Mum ____________ a message for Dad. I ____________ it down
leave write

but I think I've ____________ the piece of paper.
lose

Rule

Most nouns ending in **e** make the plural by adding **s** but some do not.

house → houses but *mouse → mice*

6 Write the plural for each noun.

table ____________ goose ____________ aeroplane ____________

fire ____________ crime ____________ man ____________

7 The words **break** and **brake** are homophones. Write the correct homophone.

Don't ____________ too quickly or you'll fall off the bike.

Don't ____________ your stride while you run.

Reflection

- I can do this.
- I am not sure.
- I need help.

Unit 2

The funny bone is not actually a bone. It is a nerve behind your elbow.

Say Listen Look Understand Remember Practise

close	______
alone	______
erode	______
suppose	______
approve	______
wardrobe	______
huge	______
pure	______
cube	______
refuse	______
accuse	______
conclude	______

1 Words can rhyme but be spelt differently. Find a list word that rhymes.

knows	toes	______
load	glowed	______
moan	blown	______
brood	glued	______
	stews	______
	groove	______

2 Use the clues to write **o-e** and **u-e** words. The mystery word is a shape.

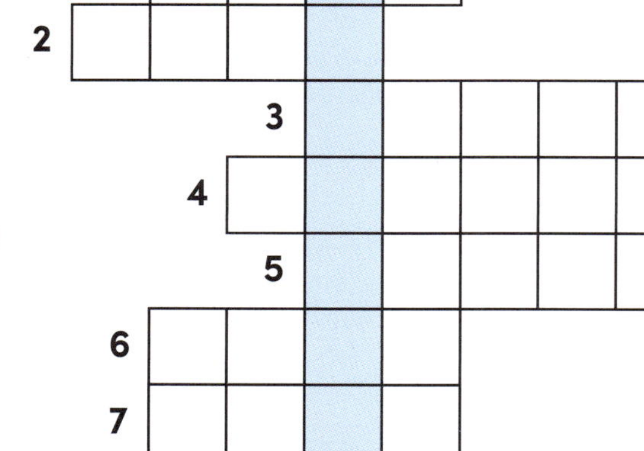

1. not spoilt or dirty
2. I _____ you!
3. Please ______ the door.
4. a piece of rock
5. all by yourself
6. Have you _____ your work?
7. very large
8. complete
9. an object with six square sides

Mystery word: ______

Spelling Rules! Student Book 3 (ISBN 9780655092698) © Janelle Ho, Helen Pearson

3 There are many ways to say *big*. Arrange these words in alphabetical order.

huge   large   gigantic   enormous   great

4 Syllables are the beats in a word. Write how many syllables you hear in each shape word.

prism  cylinder  cube  sphere 

For words that end in **e**, drop the **e** to add **ing**.

love → *loving*   *use* → *using*

Drop the **e** to add **y** to make the adjective.   *ice* → *icy*

5 Add **ing**.

close ______________ approve ______________ amaze ______________

refuse ______________ conclude ______________ promise ______________

6 Write the adjective by adding **y**.

not liking work (laze) ______________ bright, glowing (shine) ______________

having many bones, thin (bone) ______________

hard to please (choose) ______________

7 Each set of words has the same spelling pattern, but one word sounds different. Circle the word with a different sound and then use it in your own sentence.

sure pure cure	______________________________

dove love move	______________________________

Unit 3

It is easier to float in sea water than in fresh water.

Say Listen Look Understand Remember Practise	
shook	____________
blood	____________
choose	____________
soothe	____________
bleed	____________
breath	____________
breathe	____________
threat	____________
explain	____________
throat	____________
poach	____________
cockroach	____________

1 Rearrange the letters to make a list word.

ooksh	ldobo	cpoha
____________	____________	____________
soecho	rteath	theebar
____________	____________	____________
bedel	laxinep	thorta
____________	____________	____________

2 Add another word to make a compound word.

door____________ tooth____________

moon____________ ____________spoon

broom____________ ____________room

3 Write the word in the plural.

breath ____________ street ____________ tooth ____________

year ____________ goose ____________ cockroach ____________

4 Add the correct suffix to these verbs. Choose from **s**, **ed** or **ing**.

Dad is sweep____ the leaves from the driveway.

The wind blew my hat into the water. Luckily, it float____.

I hope we see a rainbow when the sun break____ through the clouds.

After our bushwalk, we feast____ on hot damper with honey.

Auntie Jean poach____ an egg for breakfast this morning.

Spelling Rules! Student Book 3 (ISBN 9780655092698) © Janelle Ho, Helen Pearson

5 These pairs of words are related: **blood–bleed**, **breath–breathe**. Which are nouns and which are verbs?

noun ______________ ______________

verb ______________ ______________

6 Write one from the pairs: **blood–bleed**, **breath–breathe**.

Be careful! If you cut yourself, you will ______________.

I think there is a lot of ______________ but Mum says it's only a tiny cut.

______________ deeply so you won't feel so out of ______________.

7 Add **e** to the noun to make the verb. Circle the parts of the word that change when you say the new word.

breath ______________ bath ______________

cloth ______________ teeth ______________

8 Colour the correct homophone.

I need | to | too | two | eggs | to | too | two | make a cake.

Cheng Mai is | to | too | two | sick to come | to | too | two | the party.

May I watch television | to | too | two |?

Foong | rowed | road | rode | ten kilometres on his bike.

Please | grate | great | the carrots.

9 Add a letter to make a new word. Use the clue! Colour the circle if the vowel sound changes.

○ heat → ______________ (grain used to make flour)

○ beat → ______________ (wild animal)

○ read → ______________ (...! Steady! Go!)

○ treat → ______________ (warning meant to frighten)

Reflection

I can do this.

I am not sure.

I need help.

Unit 4

Bamboo can grow up to 91 centimetres in one day.

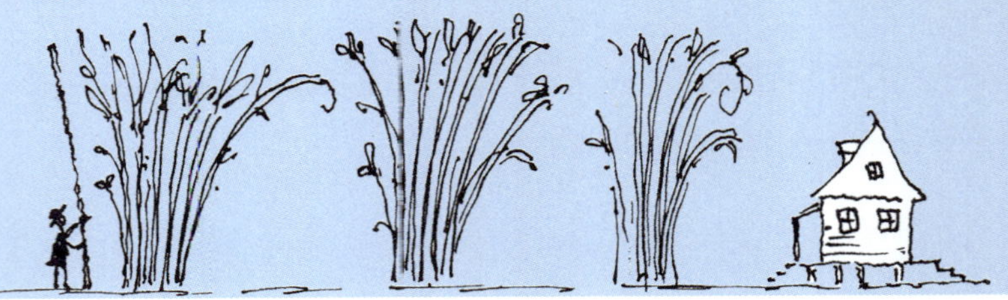

Say Listen Look Understand Remember Practise	
know	____________
growl	____________
below	____________
allow	____________
touch	____________
grouchy	____________
pounce	____________
mountain	____________
royal	____________
money	____________
trolley	____________
layer	____________

1 Write each verb in the past tense.

verb	past tense
know	
blow	
draw	
chew	
allow	

2 Write list words in the correct category.

adjective	both a noun and a verb
____________	____________
____________	____________
	____________

3 Make a new word by changing the first letter in each list word. The clues give the meaning of the new word.

list word	new word	clue
mountain	____________	water spouting
money	____________	what bees make
royal	____________	faithful
touch	____________	where a joey sleeps
growl	____________	move when hunting

4 Fill in the missing letters to name three animals.

d _ _ key m _ _ k _ _ t _ _ k _ _

Spelling Rules! Student Book 3 (ISBN 9780655092698) © Janelle Ho, Helen Pearson

5 Fill in the missing letters to make rhyming words. Add your own words.

_ _ower   _ _ower   _ower   ________

_ _own   _ _own   _ _own   ________

6 Proofread this diary entry. There are five words that are incorrect. Circle the mistakes. Then write the correct spelling of the words in the boxes.

Today Mum and I found a strey dog. The tag on his collar said he was called Honey. I made a poster and stuck it on our fence. I tied a rope to Honey's collar and we walked around the block. At first he was growchy. Then he tried to run a way. Mum's phone rang. It was Honey's owner. When she collected him, she offered me some mony but I refused. We all enjoyd seeing Honey jump up to proudly walk off with his owner.

7 Unjumble these letters. The words are all days of the week. Remember to use a capital letter.

difray ________ dratyusa ________

saddenwey ________ trayshud ________

manyod ________ yestuda ________

Which day haven't you used? ________

8 Say each word. Circle one word with a different vowel sound.

south	grouch	proud
found	pout	mouth
touch	ounce	blouse

Reflection

I can do this.

I am not sure.

I need help.

Unit 5

Cows can fall **a**sleep standing up.

Say Listen Look Understand Remember Practise

across ______
always ______
about ______
around ______
almost ______
already ______
ahead ______
asleep ______
above ______
another ______
along ______
altogether ______

1 Write a list word that means the opposite.

behind ______
below ______
separately ______
never ______
awake ______

2 Colour the circle if the **a** at the beginning has a short sound. Underline the first syllable.

alive	○	after	○
again	○	along	○
almost	○	away	○
across	○	alike	○
always	○	aloud	○

Tip A **prefix** is a syllable added at the beginning of a word to change the meaning. **un** and **dis** both give the word an opposite meaning.
kind → unkind *approve → disapprove*

3 Add **un** or **dis** at the beginning to make a word with the opposite meaning.

______happy ______safe ______obey ______known
______agree ______tidy ______like ______trust

4 Write your own words beginning with **un** or **dis**.

un______ un______ dis______

Spelling Rules! Student Book 3 (ISBN 9780655092698) © Janelle Ho, Helen Pearson

5 Arrange these words from least often to most often.

sometimes always often never rarely

____

6 Write list words.

This pen doesn't work. Can you pass me ____________ one?

We started our sport lesson by running ____________ the oval.

Hurry up! It's ____________ two o'clock.

My cat can walk ____________ the top of the fence.

We rowed ____________ the river for a picnic.

Tip

A long path is not the same as *along the path*.
Remember to leave a space between each word in a sentence.

7 Write these sentences, leaving spaces between each word.

Donotbeafraid. ______________________________

Mybrotherisawaysicktoday. ______________________________

Jackisaloneinthehouse. ______________________________

Mytwinsistersliketodressalike. ______________________________

8 Write your own beginning for a fairy tale. Use as many list words as you can.

Once upon a time ______________________________

____

____

____

____

____

Reflection

I can do this.

I am not sure.

I need help.

Unit 6 Revision

Some leeches can suck out ten times their own weight in human blood.

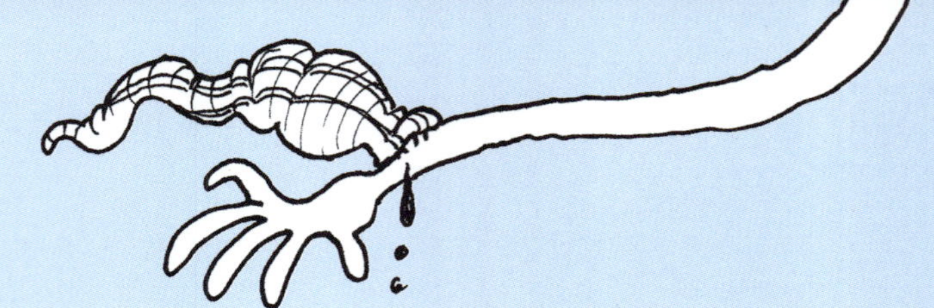

1 Add a letter to make a new word.

too ____________ lose ____________ way ____________

pant ____________ lie ____________ sleep ____________

2 Colour the correct word.

My pyjamas have red and white [strips | stripes].

We wrote the shopping list on a [scrap | scrape] of paper.

Do you like playing [hid | hide] and seek?

'Put your homework in the [tub | tube] on my desk,' said the teacher.

3 Write the correct homophone.

to too two

Omar drew a person with __________ eyes but three noses!

Kelly loves going __________ the movies when it is raining.

Bill has red hair. His twin sister does __________.

brake break

If you ____________ anything, you'll have to pay for it.

Remember to ____________ as you near the corner.

4 Colour the correct form of the verb.

I [hope | hoped] the test wouldn't be hard, but it was!

Sam [did | done] his homework before playing hockey.

Kelly [loves | loved] going to the movies when it is raining.

It was Mum's birthday, so I [make | made] her a cake.

Everyone [know | knew] about the party except Dad.

5 Write **ee** or **ea** to complete these words.

p _ _ ch	str _ _ t	scr _ _ m	cl _ _ n	sl _ _ p
tr _ _	dr _ _ m	j _ _ ns	fr _ _	_ _ t

6 Write **oa** or **ow** to complete these words.

gr _ _	fl _ _ ted	bel _ _	sh _ _ ed	l _ _ d
kn _ _	pill _ _	f _ _ m	wind _ _	sl _ _

7 Write **ou** or **ow** to complete these words.

sh _ _ t	cl _ _ n	fr _ _ n	c _ _ nt	f _ _ nd
br _ _ n	pr _ _ d	r _ _ nd	dr _ _ ned	cr _ _ n

8 Choose a word to fit each space.

above another across around almost already

Tim's best friend is Sandra, who lives ____________ the road. They play together ____________ every day. Last weekend they went to the park to play cricket. Sandra kept hitting the ball high ____________ Tim's head. He had to run a long way after it. Tim asked his older brother Toby to be fielder so he wouldn't have to keep running ____________ after the ball. Sandra hit the next ball high in the air and Toby caught it!

'Give me ____________ chance, will you?' asked Sandra.

The boys laughed and said it was now her turn to get some exercise. They had ____________ run a long way!

Spelling Rules! Student Book 3 (ISBN 9780655092698) © Janelle Ho, Helen Pearson

Unit 7

A human can live without a stomach.

Say Listen Look Understand Remember Practise	
school	____________
ache	____________
echo	____________
choir	____________
character	____________
chorus	____________
chameleon	____________
stomach	____________
monarch	____________
anchor	____________
chef	____________
machine	____________

1 Sort the list words into the correct group.

2 Write the plural.

one choir, two ____________

one character, two ____________

one chorus, two ____________

one ache, two ____________

one machine, two ____________

one chef, two ____________

3 Say each list word. Write the list words that have two syllables.

____________ ____________ ____________ ____________

____________ ____________ ____________

4 Use the clue to write a list word.

a person in a story ____________

an animal ____________

two words about singing ____________ ____________

a place that has 'cool' inside ____________

something that rumbles when you're hungry ____________

a good person to have around when you're hungry ____________

5 Make compound words.

 + ache = ____________

 + ache = ____________

 + ache = ____________

 + ache = ____________

 **6** The spaces in the sentence are in the wrong place. Write each sentence correctly.

If yout urnt o you rright and cal lout, youw ill he arane cho.

____

The bo atco ul dnot movebe ca use thes ail orf orgo ttor ais eth eanc hor!

____

 **7** What are you looking forward to in the school holidays?

____

____

____

____

____

____

Reflection

I can do this.
I am not sure.
I need help.

Unit 8

An elephant's trunk has more than 40 000 muscles – more than in a human's whole body!

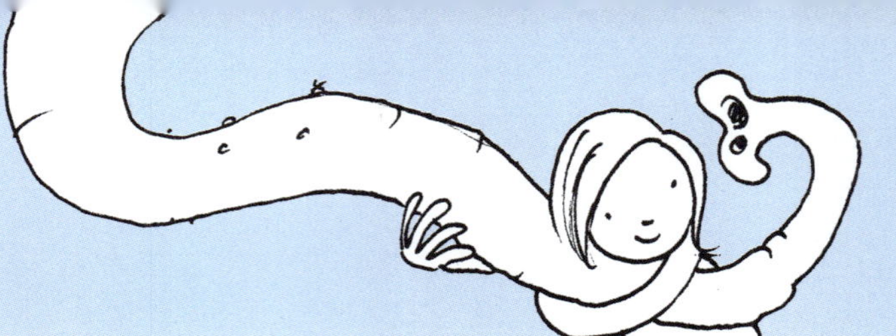

Say Listen Look Understand Remember Practise

country	________
state	________
northern	________
western	________
south	________
capital	________
territory	________
Australia	________
New South Wales	
________	
Victoria	________
Tasmania	________
Queensland	________

1 You have written a letter to your school principal. Follow the example and address the envelope correctly.

Ms R Smith
Rosehill State School
16 Howard Street
Rosehill, Tasmania 4981

____
____
____
____

2 Fill in the missing letters. Make sure each word begins with a capital letter.

_ e _ _ o _ _ h _ a _ _ s

_ ic _ _ _ i _

T _ _ _ a _ _ _

Q _ e _ _ s _ _ _ d

N _ _ th _ _ n T _ _ ri _ ory

S _ _ t _ _ u _ _ r _ _ _ _

W _ _ _ er _ _ _ s _ _ a _ _ _

_ _ _ t _ _ l _ _ n C _ pi _ _ l _ er _ _ t _ _ y

3 Join each capital city to its state or territory.

Melbourne	Western Australia	Sydney	Northern Territory
Perth	Tasmania	Brisbane	New South Wales
Hobart	South Australia	Darwin	Australian Capital Territory
Adelaide	Victoria	Canberra	Queensland

Spelling Rules! Student Book 3 (ISBN 9780655092698) © Janelle Ho, Helen Pearson

4 Choose a word to fit each space.

northern
eastern
southern
western

Brisbane and Sydney are ________________ capitals.

The most ________________ capital is Hobart.

Perth is the most ________________ capital, while the most ________________ capital is Darwin.

5 The days of the week are all proper nouns. Write the days in order.

________________ was the day of the sun.

________________ was the day of the moon.

________________ was Tiw's day. Tiw was the Norse god of war.

________________ was Woden's day. Woden was the chief Norse god.

________________ was Thor's day. Thor was the Norse god of thunder.

________________ was Frigga's day. Frigga was the chief Norse goddess.

________________ was Saturn's day. Saturn was the Roman god of farming.

Apostrophes can show that someone owns something.

Tim's bag.

6 Use the person's name and **'s** to show who owns each object.

The book belongs to Ari. It is ____________.

The coat belongs to Pia. It is ____________.

The shoes belong to Steve. They are ____________.

The scarf belongs to Mum. It is ____________.

7 Circle the letters that should be written as capitals.

cassie goes to epping for gym training every friday.

the tasman sea separates australia and new zealand.

captain cook's ship was called endeavour.

Playing a **yidaki** can help you breathe better! **Deadly**!

Say Listen Look Understand Remember Practise

Mob	______
Elder	______
Aunty	______
Uncle	______
deadly	______
gammon	______
tucker	______
humpy	______
yakka	______
yidaki	______
boomerang	______
marngrook	______

1 Write the list words in alphabetical order.

______ ______ ______

______ ______ ______

______ ______ ______

______ ______ ______

2 Say each list word. Write the words that answer the questions.

Which word has one syllable? ______

Which words have three syllables?

______ ______

Which words begin with a vowel sound?

______ ______ ______

Tip

Some words can be written in both lower case and upper case (capital letters). *aunty Aunty uncle Uncle*

When a word is written with a capital letter, it is part of a name or is important in the community.

3 Choose a word to fill each gap. Write the plural.

Mob	Elder	Aunty	Uncle

Aboriginal people belong to ______. Each Mob is linked to a place or Country. The ______ are responsible for teaching the stories of their people. They are made up of respected women and men in the community. They are known as ______ and ______.

Spelling Rules! Student Book 3 (ISBN 9780655092698) © Janelle Ho, Helen Pearson

4 Write a list word.

______________ ______________

______________ ______________

______________ ______________

5 Use the clues to write a list word.

very good ______________

fake or pretend ______________

food ______________

temporary shelter ______________

respected member of an Aboriginal community ______________

6 Add **er** or **est**.

The Aboriginal peoples have the ______________ culture in the world.
(old)

Uluru is the ______________ rock monolith in the world.
(large)

Did you know that Darwin is both the ______________ and ______________ city in Australia?
(sunny) (wet)

Tip Some **adjectives** change when you use them to compare different things.

good → *better* → *best*   *bad* → *worse* → *worst*

7 Choose the word that fits each sentence.

I am good at high jump but I'm ______________ at long jump.

I am bad at breast stroke but I'm ______________ at backstroke.

Osman sang a solo at the concert as he is the ______________ singer in our class.

I don't like it when my sister makes dinner. She is the ______________ cook I know.

8 The adjective *nice* is used too often. Find a better word for each sentence.

My cousin is very nice. ______________

This cake is nice. ______________

Reflection

- I can do this.
- I am not sure.
- I need help.

Unit 10

People used to believe the Earth was flat, and that if you walked far enough, you'd fall off!

Say Listen Look Understand Remember Practise

grief ____________
relief ____________
fierce ____________
niece ____________
sieve ____________
thieve ____________
believe ____________
friend ____________
weird ____________
receive ____________
ceiling ____________
foreign ____________

1 Find a list word that rhymes.

leaf	peeling	crease
____________	____________	____________
leave	mend	beard
____________	____________	____________

2 Write a list word for each clue.

not native ____________

the daughter of your brother or sister ____________

a container with holes ____________

sadness ____________

steal ____________

accept ____________

3 Make another ie word by changing one letter.

pierce	relieve	grief	niece
____________	____________	____________	____________

4 Follow the example to complete the table.

noun	verb	sentence (using either word)
grief	grieve	My neighbour cried with grief when his dog died.
	relieve	
belief		
thief		

Spelling Rules! Student Book 3 (ISBN 9780655092698) © Janelle Ho, Helen Pearson

5 Use the clues to complete the words. Colour the word with **ie**.

Clue					
a caterpillar's favourite food			E		F
the top of a house		R			F
the person in charge			I		F
meat from a cow				E	F
not able to hear		D			F
bread is baked in this shape		L			F
1 ÷ 2 =				L	F
a game played with a club		G			F
a flat surface to put things on			E		F
a dangerous hunting animal		W			F

Learn these homophones:

piece = a part
peace = not at war

cheap = not expensive
cheep = sound of a bird

steel = type of metal
steal = thieve or rob

6 Colour the correct word.

Jack tried to [steel | steal] a [piece | peace] of cake.

Everyone wants to live in [piece | peace].

The chicks [cheap | cheep] noisily when they are hungry.

Movie tickets are [cheap | cheep] on Tuesdays.

7 Find a list word that belongs to each group.

steal	burgle	______________	mate	buddy	______________
cousin	nephew	______________	wall	floor	______________
odd	strange	______________	scary	wild	______________

8 Write one sentence using both words.

friend piece	____ ____

Reflection

I can do this.
I am not sure.
I need help.

Unit 11

When you sneeze, air and snot fly out of your nose at 160 km/h. **Dis**gusting!

Say **L**isten **L**ook **U**nderstand **R**emember **P**ractise

untidy	________
unlikely	________
mischief	________
misplace	________
misbehave	________
mistake	________
disagree	________
disgrace	________
disgusting	________
dishonest	________
disobey	________
discover	________

1 Make a word that means the opposite by adding **un**, **mis** or **dis** at the beginning.

____lucky	____agree
____behave	____safe
____healthy	____honest
____appear	____understand
____obey	____tidy
____place	____true
____likely	____like

2 Give each sentence the opposite meaning by adding **un**, **mis** or **dis**.

The sun appeared over the horizon.

____

Your desk is so tidy!

____

Sam really likes pumpkin.

____

I agree with you.

____

The train is likely to arrive on time.

____

Spelling Rules! Student Book 3 (ISBN 9780655092698) © Janelle Ho, Helen Pearson

Synonyms are words with the same meaning.
Small and *little* are synonyms.

3 Find list words that are synonyms for these words.

error ______________ find ______________

lose ______________ messy ______________

gross ______________ trouble ______________

4 Jarrad's bedroom is a mess. Describe each object using an adjective that rhymes with the clue. Then use a list word to comment on the mess.

Jarrad's shiny bike helmet is on the floor. How untidy!
(tiny)

His __________ socks are under the bed. How __________!
(jelly)

His __________ football is on his pillow. What a __________!
(thirty)

His __________ jacket is hanging behind the door. How __________!
(blue)

When you add a prefix, do not remove any letters. If the prefix ends in the same letter the base word starts with, keep both letters.

un + noticed ⟶ *unnoticed*

dis + similar ⟶ *dissimilar*

5 Write the prefix and the base word.

misspell = _____ + __________ unnoticeable = _____ + __________

unnecessary = _____ + __________ misshape = _____ + __________

dissatisfied = _____ + __________ unnamed = _____ + __________

6 Use your dictionary to find the word meanings. Use both words in one sentence.

dismay mishap	______________________________ ______________________________

Reflection

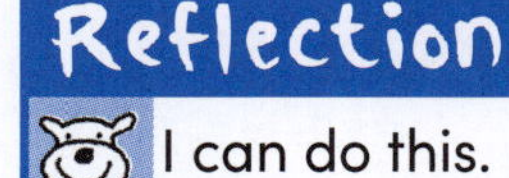

I can do this.

I am not sure.

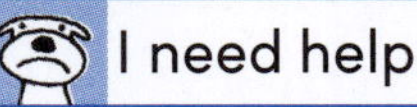

I need help.

Unit 12 Revision

It is **impossible** to lick your own elbow!

1 Complete the tables.

word	add er	add est
big		
wide		
quiet		
pretty		

word	add ly
quick	
safe	
friend	
happy	

word	add ed	add ing
smile		
groan		
drop		
worry		

word	add y
wind	
health	
dream	
mess	

2 Make a new word by adding a prefix from the shape.

un dis mis

______loyal   ______natural   ______appear   ______cover

______agree   ______behave   ______likely   ______known

3 Fill in the missing vowels.

bel_ _ve   disapp_ _nt   fr_ _nd   disapp_ _r

disagr_ _   misch_ _f   qu_ _tly   f_ _rce

empt_ _d   l_ _dly   p_ _ceful   _ _str_l_a

Spelling Rules! Student Book 3 (ISBN 9780655092698) © Janelle Ho, Helen Pearson

 Add a letter to the beginning of each word to make a new word.

_ lean	_ nail	_ rail	_ tone	_ room
_ rain	_ lower	_ new	_ now	_ rush
_ heat	_ harm	_ rack	_ rust	_ lack

 Circle the letters that should be written as capitals. Add capital letters and apostrophes.

my name is ahmed and im afraid of snakes. i live in alice springs and i know there are plenty of snakes out there.

last sunday i was sitting outside reading charlottes web by e.b white. mum called me and i looked up. there it was. a python. mum is a vet and is used to handling snakes. she picked up the python and popped it into my brothers gym bag. i breathed again. its a good thing she was home.

6 Match the capital city to its traditional place name.

Canberra	Yuggera
Melbourne	Nipaluna
Brisbane	Eora
Darwin	Larrakia
Sydney	Ngunnawal
Hobart	Woiworung
Perth	Wajuk

7 Use your dictionary.

What is the next word after stork?

____

What is the word before toast?

____

Arrange in alphabetical order:
strong, stale, stink, stupid, stage

______________ ______________

______________ ______________

____

Unit 13

Meerkats are very help**ful** animals. They often take care of each other's babies.

Say Listen Look Understand Remember Practise	
help**ful**	______
aw**ful**	______
harm**ful**	______
peace**ful**	______
colour**ful**	______
grate**ful**	______
beauti**ful**	______
help**less**	______
use**less**	______
care**less**	______
fear**less**	______
life**less**	______

1 Add the suffix.

joy, cheer, watch, use, peace → ful

______
______
______
______
______

care, hope, blame, help, harm → less

______
______
______
______
______

Tip The suffixes **ful** and **less** usually make the new words **antonyms**. Antonyms are words that are opposite in meaning.

2 Make antonyms.

use	______	______	care	______	______
harm	______	______	pain	______	______
colour	______	______	joy	______	______

3 Some words add **ful** but not **less**. Circle these in blue. Others add **less** but not **ful**. Circle these in red.

play	life	blame	plenty
boast	beauty	face	hand

Spelling Rules! Student Book 3 (ISBN 9780655092698) © Janelle Ho, Helen Pearson

If a word ends in **y**, change **y** to **i** before adding **ful** or **less**.

duty → dutiful

4 Write the word.

beauty + ful → ______________ mercy + less → ______________

pity + less → ______________ plenty + ful → ______________

5 Use the clue to find a list word to fit each sentence.

I sprained my ankle because I was ______________. (not paying attention)

Aunty was ______________ in facing the bullies. (brave)

Our classroom is bright and ______________. (has many colours)

'Thank you! I am ______________ you could help.' (glad)

Did you see the ______________ sunrise this morning? (pretty)

I baked the cake without sugar. It tasted ______________. (bad)

Belle's description of her character was ______________ so she rewrote it. (dull)

We were shocked when a fight broke out on our ______________ street. (quiet)

6 Words for quantities sometimes end in **ful**. *Handful* is an example. Use the pictures as clues to write these quantities.

______________ ______________ ______________

______________ ______________ ______________

7 Write your own sentence using these words.

awful	______________
wonderful	______________

Reflection

- I can do this.
- I am not sure.
- I need help.

The first sausage may have been made more than 5000 years ago! Awesome!

Say Listen Look Understand Remember Practise	
taut	____________
haul	____________
fault	____________
pause	____________
sauce	____________
sausage	____________
audio	____________
flaw	____________
thaw	____________
drawer	____________
sprawl	____________
awesome	____________

1 Write **au** or **aw**.

l _ _	dr _ _	bec _ _ se
t _ _ t	s _ _ ce	_ _ ful
y _ _ n	_ _ dio	h _ _ l
p _ _ se	th _ _	r _ _

2 Write a list word.

____________ ____________ ____________

3 Add a suffix to make a word family. Not all suffixes will be used.

Base word	add s	add ed	add ing
haul			
fault			
pause			
sausage		X	X
flaw			X
thaw			
drawer		X	X
sprawl			

4 Write a list word that rhymes.

salt	crawl	shores	door	four
______	______	______	______	______

All the words have the same vowel sound. Write all the ways to make this sound.

____

 Unscramble the letters to make a word.

wraedr	iodua	pwarls	oasweem	gaseusa
______	______	______	______	______

 Choose the correct homophone.

The lions [raw | roar] once they smell the [raw | roar] [meat | meet].

Mr Paul's shoulder is still [saw | sore]. He hurt the muscle when he tried out his [new | knew] [saw | sore].

Oh no! Did Shaun [draw | drawer] all over the [blew | blue] [draws | drawers]? No. He [threw | through] finger paint on the [flaw | floor].

[Paw | Poor | Pour] some milk into the dish for the [paw | poor | pour] cat.

 Synonyms are words with the same meaning. Antonyms are words with opposite meanings. Write a list word.

synonym	list word	antonym
tight	______	loose
melt	______	freeze
rest	______	continue
amazing	______	boring
______	______	virtue

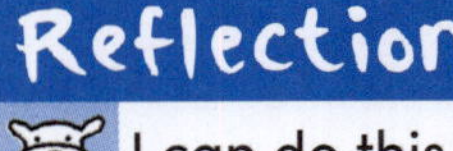

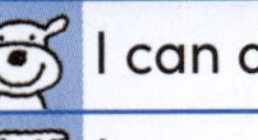 I can do this.

I am not sure.

I need help.

Spelling Rules! Student Book 3 (ISBN 9780655092698) © Janelle Ho, Helen Pearson

Unit 15

When a horse ga**ll**ops, all four hooves are off the ground at once.

Say **L**isten **L**ook **U**nderstand **R**emember **P**ractise

ga**ll**op	______
co**ll**ide	______
tu**nn**el	______
cha**nn**el	______
te**nn**is	______
ru**bb**ish	______
co**mm**on	______
le**ss**on	______
bo**rr**ow	______
qua**rr**el	______
a**ff**ect	______
e**ff**ect	______

1 The words in each ladder are missing the same double letters. Write the missing letters.

ga _ _ op
pi _ _ ow
ba _ _ oon
ye _ _ ow

ss
tt
nn
ll

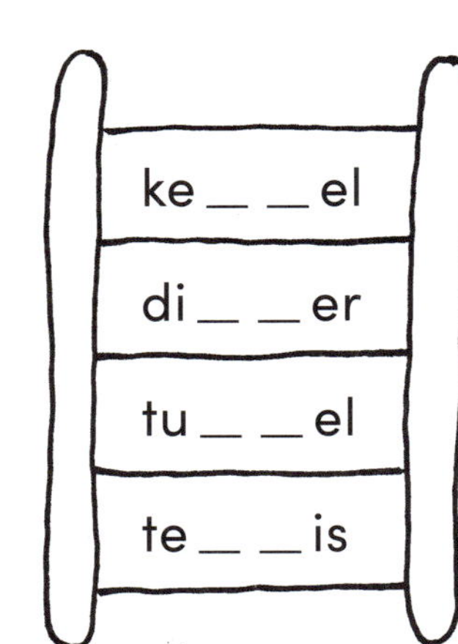

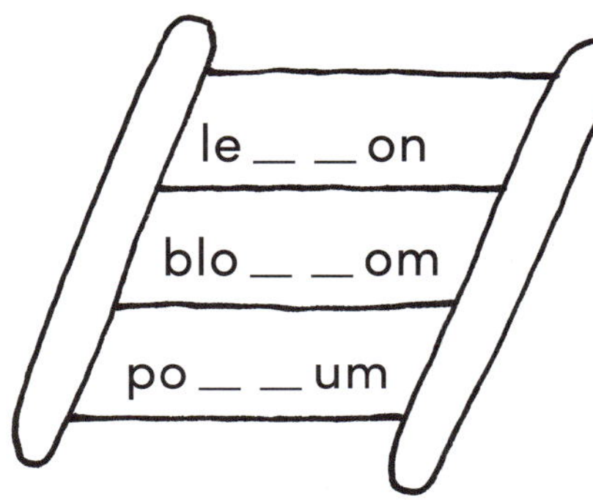

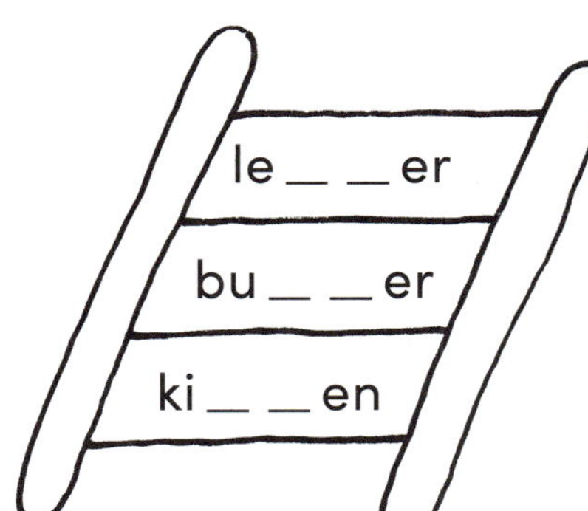

2 Use the clue to complete each word.

_ ff _ _ _	cause a change
_ _ rr _ _	a long orange vegetable
_ _ rr _ _	what you do with books in a library
_ _ _ rr _ _	argue
_ _ mm _ _	a tool for hitting nails
_ _ mm _ _	shared by everyone
_ _ dd _ _	useful for reaching high places
_ _ ll _ _ _	crash together
_ _ bb _ _ _	litter
_ pp _ _ _	opposite of vanish

The words **affect** and **effect** are often confused.
affect (verb) = cause a change
effect (noun) = result of a change

3 Write the correct word. You may need to add a suffix.

The assembly talk had a positive ______________ on the students.

The noise is ______________ Billy's ability to focus.

For our science project, we learned how light ______________ plants.

One ______________ is that plants grow towards light.

4 Choose one word from each box to make compound words.

letter	wheel	grass	button	pillow	bitter
hopper	box	hole	sweet	barrow	case

______________ ______________ ______________

______________ ______________ ______________

5 Circle the words that need double letters and write them correctly.

We never leave rubish in our backyard. But last night my dog, Oscar, knocked over the bin and the lid came of. A posum colected some stale bread and buter and ate it for diner. Then it started to galop noisily over our roof. Dad used a lader to climb up and shoo it away. I tied Oscar in his kenel as he was trying to burow under the fence. He quickly slipped out of his colar and ran away. What a busy night!

______________ ______________

______________ ______________

______________ ______________

____

____

____

____

____

Reflection

- I can do this.
- I am not sure.
- I need help.

Unit 16

The first bubblegum was made in ancient Greece from tree resin.

Say Listen Look Understand Remember Practise	
apple	______
saddle	______
puddle	______
riddle	______
cuddle	______
bubble	______
bottle	______
kettle	______
little	______
juggle	______
giggle	______
wriggle	______

1 Write the double letters.

pu _ _ le
wri _ _ le
cu _ _ le
bu _ _ le
bo _ _ le
li _ _ le
fi _ _ le

ke _ _ le
sa _ _ le
wo _ _ le
gi _ _ le
ri _ _ le
ju _ _ le
pe _ _ le

2 Change one letter to make a new word.

riddle (m) ______
puddle (a) ______
giggle (j) ______

juggle (str) ______
bottle (a) ______
middle (f) ______

3 Make new words by adding **le** to these words.

buck ______
pick ______
chuck ______
trick ______

tick ______
crack ______
tack ______
suck ______

sing ______
tang ______
bang ______

The **k** in **kn** is a silent letter. *knuckle*
The **w** in **wr** is a silent letter. *wriggle*

Fill in the missing silent letter. Choose **k** or **w**.

_nee

_nuckle

_rite

_rist

_rong

_not

_nife

_nit

_riggle

Here are some interesting words to use instead of *talk*. Write the words in the correct speech bubble.

jabber	bellow	mutter	shout
whisper	gabble	roar	mumble
shriek	murmur	babble	chatter

talk loudly

______
______
______
______

talk quietly

______ ______
______ ______

talk quickly

______
______
______
______

Fill in the letters to complete the word.

Viv set _ _ _ d down to nib _ _ _ her ap _ _ _.

Bob drib _ _ _ d some water from his bot _ _ _. It made a lit _ _ _ pud _ _ _.

Fill in missing vowels so that these words are in alphabetical order.

scr_bble scr_mble scr_bble sc_ffle sc_ttle

Reflection

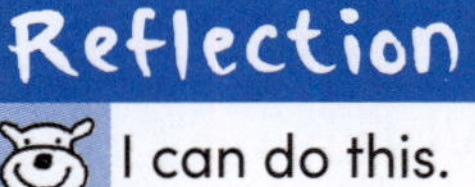

I can do this.
I am not sure.
I need help.

Unit 17

The Roman emperor Julius Caesar named the month of July after himself.

Say Listen Look Understand Remember Practise

January __________
February __________
March __________
April __________
May __________
June __________
July __________
August __________
September __________
October __________
November __________
December __________

1 Unjumble the letters for each month. Don't forget to start with a capital letter!

luyj	jurayan
__________	__________
bemveron	aym
__________	__________
tugusa	fryubare
__________	__________
recembed	charm
__________	__________
enju	brotoce
__________	__________
perbmeets	prail
__________	__________

2 How many days are there in each month? Use the number clues to complete this rhyme.

Clue: January = 1 December = 12

Thirty days have __________ (9), __________ (4), __________ (6)

and __________ (11).

All the rest have thirty-one,

Except for __________ (2) alone

Which has twenty-eight days clear

And twenty-nine in each leap year!

Spelling Rules! Student Book 3 (ISBN 9780655092698) © Janelle Ho, Helen Pearson

3 Write the months that match each season. Which is your favourite month? Why?

summer	autumn	winter	spring

My favourite month is ______________________________

____

Proper nouns name people, places, pets, days of the week, months, books and poems. Proper nouns are always written with a capital letter.

 **4** Circle the nouns that need capital letters in these sentences.

My uncle josh is driving his caravan from sydney to perth next july.

It was my birthday last friday and grandad gave me a book about mt everest.

easter sunday moves each year but is always in march or april.

 **5** Write a sentence using as many proper nouns as you can that begin with the same letter.

Jillian Jones, who was born in January, lives on Jack Street in Jindabyne.

____

____

 **6** Complete the table to build word families.

noun	adjective	compound word or noun group
	daily	daytime
week		
		lunar month
		leap year

Unit 18 Revision

The bigg**est** frog in the world is the Goliath frog. A Goliath frog can weigh as much as a house cat!

1 These words all have one or two prefixes or suffixes. Write the base words to which the prefixes and suffixes were added. Underline the prefixes and suffixes.

unhelpful ______________ littlest ______________ burrowed ______________

awfully ______________ guessing ______________ disappear ______________

returned ______________ bravely ______________ replied ______________

beginning ______________ pitiless ______________ beautiful ______________

2 Add the prefix or suffix shown to each base word.

empty + ed ______________

juggle + ing ______________

hope + less ______________

worry + ed ______________

un + marry + ed ______________

win + er ______________

dis + agree + s ______________

pain + ful + ly ______________

pretty + est ______________

mis + understand ______________

fear + ful + ly ______________

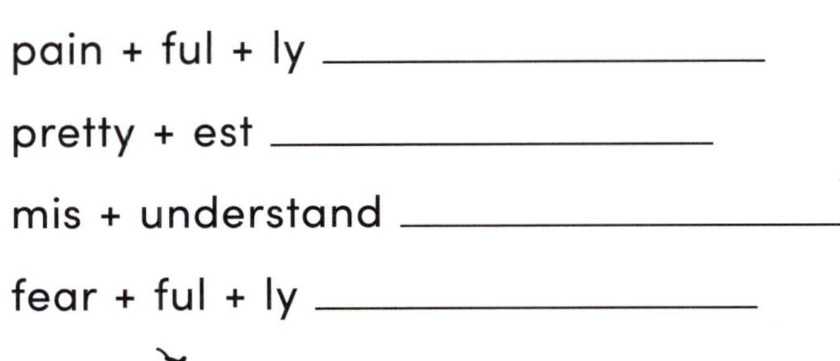

Rule Two-syllable words with a double consonant break into syllables between the consonants.

puddle = pud/dle *tennis = ten/nis* *possum = pos/sum*

3 Mark the syllable breaks in these words. In the circle, write the number of syllables you hear.

January ◯ April ◯ July ◯

giggle ◯ wriggled ◯ middle ◯

balloon ◯ rubbish ◯ bubbling ◯

playfully ◯ colourful ◯ summer ◯

Spelling Rules! Student Book 3 (ISBN 9780655092698) © Janelle Ho, Helen Pearson

Antonyms are words with the opposite meaning.
Big and *little* are antonyms.
Antonyms are also formed using prefixes and suffixes.
kind ***un**kind* *harm**ful*** *harm**less***

4 Write an antonym for each of these words.

hard ____________ long ____________ peaceful ____________
tidy ____________ end ____________ painful ____________
obey ____________ ugly ____________ honest ____________

5 Where does each animal live?

dog ____________ horse ____________ wombat ____________
rabbit ____________ bird ____________ pig ____________
goldfish ____________ bee ____________ owl ____________
sheep____________ worm ____________

6 Make a new word by adding a consonant at the beginning. Can you add two?

_tale _each _our _harp _ear
_nail _port _lame _lean _are

7 Make a new word by adding a letter at the end.

ski_ she_ rid_ was_ pea_
not_ dam_ grin_ bat_ win_

8 Make a new word by adding an extra vowel.

pin ____________ man ____________ shut ____________
bat ____________ flat ____________ rod ____________

Unit 19

Gorillas can be **taught** to use sign language to communicate with people.

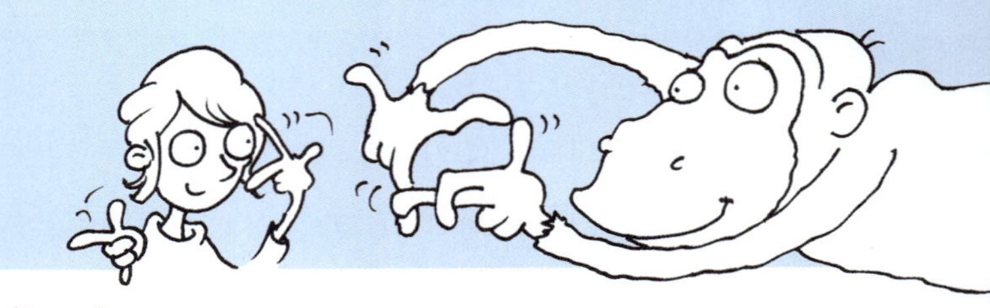

Say Listen Look Understand Remember Practise	
midn**igh**t	________
fr**igh**ten	________
n**eigh**bour	________
r**ough**	________
en**ough**	________
th**ough**	________
thr**ough**	________
th**ough**t	________
c**augh**t	________
t**augh**t	________
d**augh**ter	________
n**augh**ty	________

1 Write **ei**, **ou** or **au**.

c _ _ gh
c _ _ ght
en _ _ gh
d _ _ ghter
t _ _ gh
thr _ _ gh
_ _ ght
w _ _ ght
t _ _ ght
th _ _ gh
r _ _ gh
b _ _ ght
n _ _ ghty
n _ _ gh

Most verbs show the past tense by adding **ed**.

discover → discovered

Irregular verbs have a different form in the past tense.

write → wrote *throw → threw*

2 Complete the tables.

verb	past tense
buy	
cough	
teach	

verb	past tense
think	
fight	
weigh	

3 Choose the right word for each space.

tough though through thought

I cut ________ the steak but it was too ________ to chew.

Even ________ it was sunny, I ________ it might rain later.

It was ________ to train the lion to jump ________ the burning hoop.

Spelling Rules! Student Book 3 (ISBN 9780655092698) © Janelle Ho, Helen Pearson

Remember! **Antonyms** are words with the opposite meaning.

day, night *easy, difficult* *high, low*

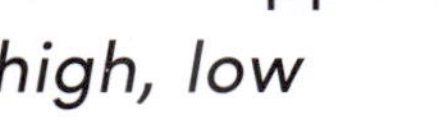

  Write a list word that is an antonym.

good ______________ threw ______________

smooth ______________ learned ______________

 Circle the words that don't make sense. Write another word so that the passage makes sense.

It was midday on Christmas Eve. As there was no moon it was very dark. Sam knew it was naughty but he fought to stay asleep. He once dreamed he had caught Santa Claus delivering presents. There was a soft crash outside and Sam jumped out of bed to shine his torch through the window. Two dull shiny eyes blinked, then disappeared. It was just a possum. Sam turned around to climb back into bed and gasped. Leaning against his bed was a tiny package. It must be the new bike he wanted. But how had it got there?

____

____

____

____

____

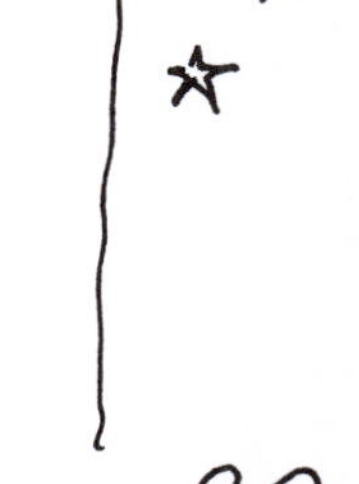

 Write a sentence using each word.

smell (noun) ______________

smell (verb) ______________

sigh (noun) ______________

sigh (verb) ______________

Reflection

I can do this.

I am not sure.

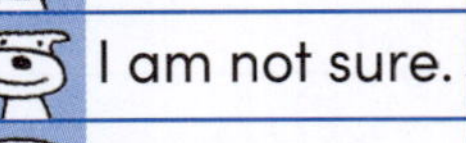

I need help.

Spelling Rules! Student Book 3 (ISBN 9780655092698) © Janelle Ho, Helen Pearson

Unit 20

Elephants can talk to other elephants that are kilometres away using sounds that are too low for humans to hear.

Say Listen Look Understand Remember Practise

laugh ____________
toughen ____________
graph ____________
photograph ____________
autograph ____________
elephant ____________
telephone ____________
sphere ____________
trophy ____________
alphabet ____________
phrase ____________
physical ____________

1 Say each word aloud. Circle the word if **gh** has an **f** sound.

cough	caught	rough
tough	light	laugh
height	enough	weigh
trough	drought	though

2 In text messages and emails, people sometimes write words as they sound, instead of using the correct spelling. Write each word correctly.

coff ____________ larf ____________

enuff ____________ fone ____________

3 Divide these list words into syllables. Underline the stressed syllable. Write the number of syllables in each word.

graph ○	enough ○	telephone ○	trophy ○	physical ○
sphere ○	alphabet ○	autograph ○	phrase ○	laughter ○

4 Write the list words in alphabetical order.

____

____

____

Spelling Rules! Student Book 3 (ISBN 9780655092698) © Janelle Ho, Helen Pearson

Some words are easier to understand when they are broken up into parts. Use a dictionary to find the meaning of the parts of these words. What other words do you know that start or end this way?

tele = ______________________ + phone = ______________________

The word is ______________________.

photo = ______________________ + graph = ______________________

The word is ______________________.

auto = ______________________ + graph = ______________________

The word is ______________________.

Other words: ____

6 Write list words.

The newspaper article used a ______________ to show that crime rates are falling.

Phil's favourite ______________ is 'rough and ready'.

Mia was awarded the ______________ for the best and fairest player in the netball competition.

When the peels are dried in the sun, they will ______________.

Did you know that Earth is not a perfect ______________?

7 Choose your favourite photograph. Why do you love this photo? Explain why it is meaningful.

____

____

____

____

____

____

____

____

Reflection

- I can do this.
- I am not sure.
- I need help.

Unit 21

No two giraffes have the same pattern on their skin.

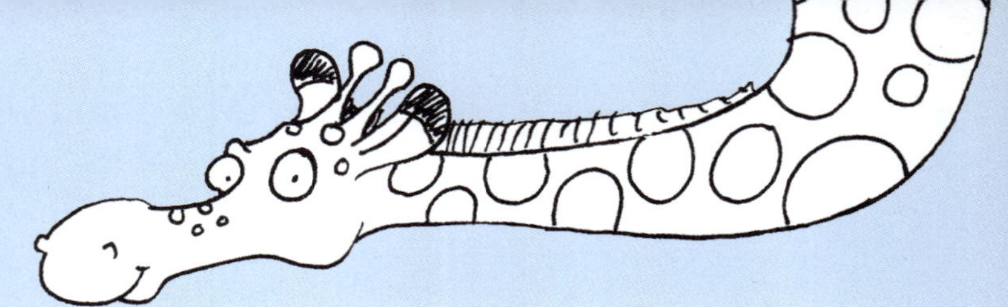

Say Listen Look Understand Remember Practise

puff	______
cliff	______
staff	______
shelf	______
wolf	______
scarf	______
wharf	______
thief	______
knife	______
handkerchief	______
yourself	______
giraffe	______

1 Find a list word that rhymes.

calf	laugh	wife
______	______	______
stiff	**leaf**	**bluff**
______	______	______

Tip

If a word ends in an **f** sound, has one syllable and a short vowel sound, it usually ends in **ff**.

stuff, off

2 Add a short vowel to make a word.

st__ff   bl__ff   sn__ff   fl__ff   h__ff   gr__ff

Rule

If a noun ends in **f** or **fe**, change the **f** or **fe** to **v** and add **es** to form the plural. *elf → elves*   *life → lives*

If a noun ends in **ff** or **ffe**, add **s** to form the plural.

3 Write the plural for each noun.

half ______	loaf ______	knife ______
puff ______	thief ______	cliff ______
yourself ______	shelf ______	giraffe ______

A **collective noun** names a group of people, animals or things.
a pod of whales *a fleet of ships* *an army of soldiers*

4 Choose an animal to complete each collective noun. Use a dictionary if you need help.

wolves kittens bees sheep cattle fish

a flock of ____________ a school of ____________

a litter of ____________ a swarm of ____________

a herd of ____________ a pack of ____________

Write one more collective noun: a______________ of ______________

Make up one yourself: a ______________ of ______________

Add a consonant to the beginning of each word to make a new word that rhymes.
ring → bring

_lane _room _rain _row _pace

_rust _lace _low _rush _win

6 Write an antonym for each clue.

A		K								
B			L							
C				H						
D					R					
E						T				
F							T			
G								Y		
H									L	
I										Y

A answer
B freeze
C throw
D safety
E hardest
F closest
G suddenly
H vertical
I patiently

Spelling Rules! Student Book 3 (ISBN 9780655092698) © Janelle Ho, Helen Pearson

Unit 22

Only female mosquit**oes** suck blood.

Say Listen Look Understand Remember Practise

her**o**	____________
pian**o**	____________
zer**o**	____________
radi**o**	____________
t**oe**	____________
can**oe**	____________
kangar**oo**	____________
tab**oo**	____________
sof**a**	____________
dram**a**	____________
ide**a**	____________
er**a**	____________

If a noun ends in **o**, you usually add **es** to make the plural.

echo → echoes

If the word comes from another language, you usually add **s** to make the plural.

avocado (Spanish) → avocados

piano (Italian) → pianos

If the word ends in two vowels, just add **s**.

radio → radios

1 Write the plural ending for these nouns.

canoe____	mosquito____	hero____
kimono____	radio____	toe____
volcano____	kangaroo____	dingo____
video____	banjo____	studio____

2 Write the plural ending for the items on this list.

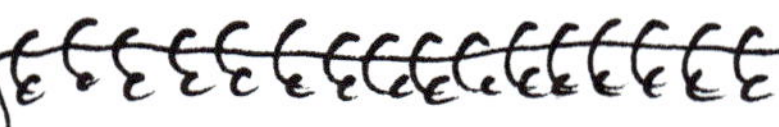

3 kg potato____

1 kg tomato____

2 mango____

2 avocado____

0.5 kg pea____

4 banana____

4 peach____

3 An abbreviation is a short form of a longer word. Use your dictionary to find the longer word for each abbreviation.

hippo	____________
rhino	____________
photo	____________
kilo	____________

Spelling Rules! Student Book 3 (ISBN 9780655092698) © Janelle Ho, Helen Pearson

4 Why is there no singular form for these words?

scissors tongs pliers trousers binoculars tweezers

All the words ____

____

 Complete the tables.

singular	plural
woman	
	mice
salmon	
	eras
cockroach	

singular	plural
photo	
	people
tooth	
	magpies
idea	

Take care with these words.
there = a place (<u>here</u> and t<u>here</u>)
their = belonging to them (It is always followed by a noun.)
they're = they are
Where are their clothes? They're over there!

6 Write your own sentences to show how each word is used.

there ____

____

their ____

____

____

they're ____

____

____

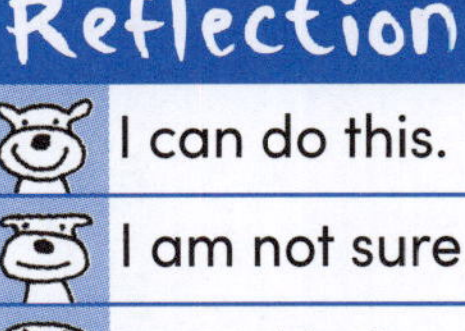

Unit 23

Sharks can't swim back**wards**.

Say Listen Look Understand Remember Practise

kind**ness**	______
happi**ness**	______
revis**ion**	______
televis**ion**	______
direct**ion**	______
friend**ship**	______
king**dom**	______
free**dom**	______
for**wards**	______
back**wards**	______
child**hood**	______
neighbour**hood**	
______	

1  Make nouns by choosing the right suffix to add to these words.

ness ship dom hood

kind______	friend______
king______	late______
dark______	loud______
child______	truthful______
bore______	free______
neighbour______	tired______
forgetful______	sponsor______
gentle______	adult______

If a word ends in **y**, change the **y** to **i** before adding **ness**.

lonely → *loneliness*

2  Add **ness** to these words.

happy	lazy	empty
______	______	______
ugly	friendly	dizzy
______	______	______

3 Name each mathematical operation. Each one ends in **ion**.

2 + 3 = 5 ______	6 − 2 = 4 ______
4 × 2 = 8 ______	6 ÷ 3 = 2 ______

Spelling Rules! Student Book 3 (ISBN 9780655092698) © Janelle Ho, Helen Pearson

Some verbs can be changed into nouns by adding **ion**.

If the verb ends in **e**, drop the **e** before adding **ion**.

confuse → confusion

4 Complete the tables.

verb	noun
act	
	separation
discuss	
	revision
connect	

verb	noun
	introduction
direct	
	explanation
televise	
	starvation

5 The suffix **wards** means *in the direction of*. Write four words that use this suffix and give the antonym for each one.

	word	antonym
in	_______________	_______________
for → wards	_______________	_______________
up	_______________	_______________

6 Make a noun by adding a suffix to the adjective. Look in a dictionary. Use both nouns in one sentence.

wise
likely

____

____

The words **revision** and **television** have the same root, **vision**, which comes from the Latin word that means *to see*.

7 What do **re** and **tele** mean?

re: ____

tele: ____

Reflection

- I can do this.
- I am not sure.
- I need help.

Tomat**oes** are really a kind of fruit, not a vegetable!

Fill in the missing vowels.

can_ _ w_ _ght r_d_ _ b_ _ght c_ _ght

Fill in the missing consonants.

ni_ _t s_a_ _ _ _i_es t_o_ _y _an_a_oo

Complete the tables.

singular	plural
canoe	
	tomatoes
hero	
	women

singular	plural
cliff	
	shelves
wharf	
	wolves

Make a new noun by adding a suffix to the base word.

king________ friend________ child________ leader________

Add suffixes to these adjectives to make adverbs and nouns.

adjective	sad	kind	happy	free	lazy
adverb					
noun					

Spelling Rules! Student Book 3 (ISBN 9780655092698) © Janelle Ho, Helen Pearson

6 Write the homophone for each word.

raw	site	threw	weight	write
______	______	______	______	______
fort	choose	wade	allowed	stares
______	______	______	______	______

7 Circle the words that are not used correctly in this story.

Last holidays, Mum bought cheep tickets to Singapore. The flight took ate hours and I had red most of my book by the time the plain landed. I couldn't sleep because as soon as we took of, a baby sitting only too rose behind us started to cry. She didn't give her parents a moment of piece the hole journey.

The whether their was hot and sticky every day, so Mum decided we should all by some knew summer clothes. When we packed to go home, our suitcase was so full I thought it might brake. It was not a problem, though, because we through out for pears of old jeans to make room.

Tip An **anagram** is formed by rearranging the letters in a word. *Lemon* is an anagram of *melon*.

8 Use the clues to make anagrams of these words.

cars ______ a mark on the skin

thorn ______ one of the points on a compass

state ______ one of the five senses

Unit 25

Snakes use their tongues to smell.

Say Listen Look Understand Remember Practise	
wrinkle	________
wrestle	________
knead	________
knowledge	________
gnaw	________
gnome	________
hour	________
honest	________
island	________
tongue	________
doubt	________
ghost	________

1 Circle the silent letter in each of these words. Write a list word with the same silent letter.

gnaw	hour
________	________
debt	listen
________	________
wrong	ghoul
________	________
rogue	knock
________	________

2 These body parts all have silent letters. Write the word.

____

____

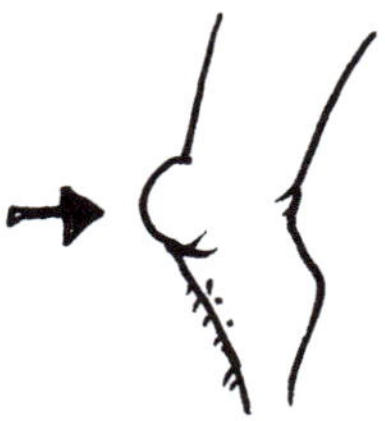

____

____

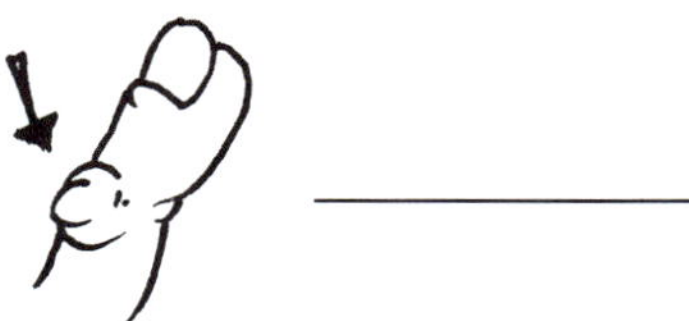

____

3 Add a suffix to each word. Circle the silent letter.

ghost + ly ________	gnaw + ing ________
wrap + ed ________	wrinkle + ing ________
doubt + ful ________	honest + y ________

Some letters can't start or end words.

- No English words begin with double consonants.
- No English words end with **q** or **v**.

These words have all come from another language. That is why the spelling looks unusual. Match each type of boat to its description. The first one has been done for you.

canoe (Spanish)	a boat with sails
kayak (Inuit)	a very small rowboat
yacht (Dutch)	a small boat with a roof made of mats
pontoon (French)	a light boat with a cover that fits around the paddler's waist
gondola (Italian)	a boat with two joined hulls
catamaran (Tamil)	a lightweight boat with paddles
dinghy (Hindi)	a boat used to support a temporary bridge
sampan (Chinese)	a long flat-bottomed boat with one oar

There are many words you can use instead of *went*.
The dog wriggled through the narrow gap in the fence.
Find a better word than *went* to complete these sentences.

The ghost ______________ through the door.

The elephant ______________ through the reeds to reach the waterhole.

Jack and Jill ______________ up the hill to fetch a pail of water.

We ______________ through the dark tunnel.

Fill in the missing vowels to make words you can use instead of *walked*.
Add four of your own. Use two of these verbs in your own sentences.

str _ d _ d _ wdl _ d t _ pt _ _ d w _ ddl _ d tr _ dg _ d

____

____

____

____

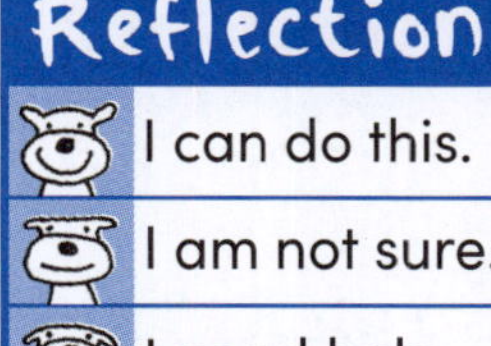

Spelling Rules! Student Book 3 (ISBN 9780655092698) © Janelle Ho, Helen Pearson

Unit 26

Australian cicadas are the loudest insects in the world.

Say Listen Look Understand Remember Practise	
carpet	______
cancel	______
once	______
lettuce	______
advice	______
cucumber	______
cylinder	______
because	______
decide	______
scent	______
science	______
scissors	______

1 Say each list word aloud and listen to the sound the **c** makes. Write the word inside the appropriate shape.

sounds like **s**

sounds like **k**

both **s** and **k** sounds

2 Look at the letters following **c** in each group of words in question 1. Fill in the missing letters for the two rules.

c is soft like **s** when the next letter is _, _ or _.

c is hard like **k** when the next letter is _, _ or _.

3 Fill in the missing letters for these vegetables. If you need help, use a dictionary.

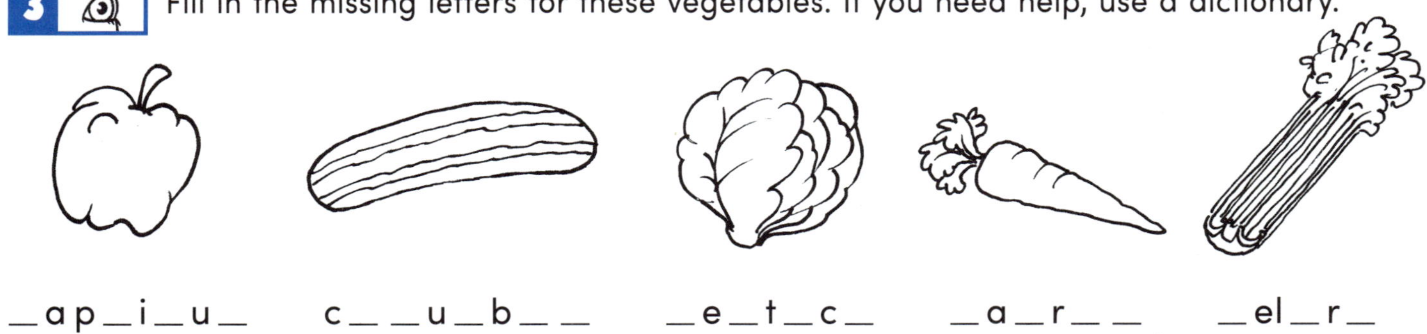

_ap_i_u_ c_ _u_b_ _ _e_t_c_ _a_r_ _ _el_r_

Spelling Rules! Student Book 3 (ISBN 9780655092698) © Janelle Ho, Helen Pearson

4 The missing letters all make an **s** sound. Write **c**, **s** or **sc**.

___ertain ___ircle ___ircu___ ___urfa___e ___issors

___entre ___ement ___ene ___eiling ___ien___e

5 The missing letters all make a **k** sound. Write **c** or **k**.

_oala _urtain _olour _ettle _upboard

_on_rete _itchen _orrect _itten ci_ada

6 Complete the crossword puzzle.

	1	2
3	4	5
6	7	8

Across

3\.

4\.

7\.

8\.

Down

1\.

2\.

5\.

6\.

7 Write your own sentences using these verbs.

inspected	________________________________
glanced	________________________________

8 Use a more interesting word than *looked* in each sentence.

The sailor ______________ at the horizon for hours.

I ______________ inside the box, hoping to find jewels and money.

Remi ______________ everywhere for his lost wallet.

Reflection

I can do this.

I am not sure.

I need help.

Unit 27

The big red spot on the planet Jupiter is a **gig**antic storm. It's three times the size of Earth, and hundreds of years old!

Say **L**isten **L**ook **U**nderstand **R**emember **P**ractise

gather	____________
guest	____________
guide	____________
to**g**ether	____________
germ	____________
gentle	____________
genius	____________
giant	____________
lar**ge**	____________
sta**ge**	____________
gigantic	____________
gypsy	____________

1 Say each list word aloud and listen to the sound the **g** makes. Write the word inside the appropriate shape.

soft **g** as in gem

hard **g** as in gate

soft **g** and hard **g**

2 Look at the words in the gem and on the gate. Fill in the missing letters for the two rules.

g is usually soft when the next letter is _, _ or _.

g is usually hard when the next letter is _, _ or _.

3 Say these words aloud. Put a tick in the box if they follow the rules above. Put a cross in the box if they don't.

gather ☐	golf ☐	together ☐	generally ☐
giggle ☐	gaze ☐	guard ☐	gymnastics ☐

Spelling Rules! Student Book 3 (ISBN 9780655092698) © Janelle Ho, Helen Pearson

4 Make a new word by adding a suffix from the box.

ly	ed	er	th	ful	ing

grace______ guess______ grow______ great______

glad______ garden______ groan______ grin______

5 Make an adjective by adding **y**. Remember your spelling rules.

noun	adjective
greed	
gloom	
guilt	
grease	
gas	

6 Complete the table.

singular	plural
gypsy	
grocery	
guest	
genius	
gentleman	

7 Here are some interesting words you can use instead of *big* and *little*. Write the name of an animal that fits each adjective.

a gigantic ______________

a giant ______________

an enormous ______________

a huge ______________

a large ______________

a microscopic ______________

a miniscule ______________

a miniature ______________

a tiny ______________

8 Colour the correct word.

Great	Grate	the apple – not your finger!

You have | grown | groan | so tall this year.

Everyone | guest | guessed | who would win.

Reflection

I can do this.

I am not sure.

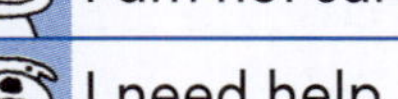

I need help.

Unit 28

In India, rubber fig trees are tied or twisted together to form living bri**dge**s. Some are more than 50 metres long!

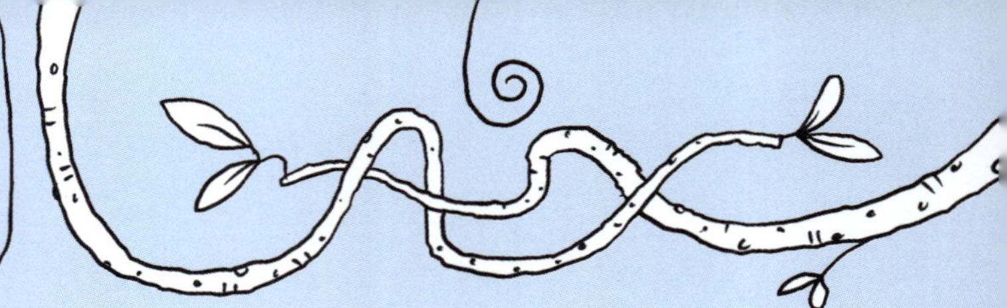

Say Listen Look Understand Remember Practise	
e**dge**	______
he**dge**	______
ba**dge**	______
fri**dge**	______
bri**dge**	______
ju**dge**	______
nu**dge**	______
tru**dge**	______
smu**dge**	______
do**dge**	______
fi**dge**t	______
ga**dge**t	______

1 Write the words.

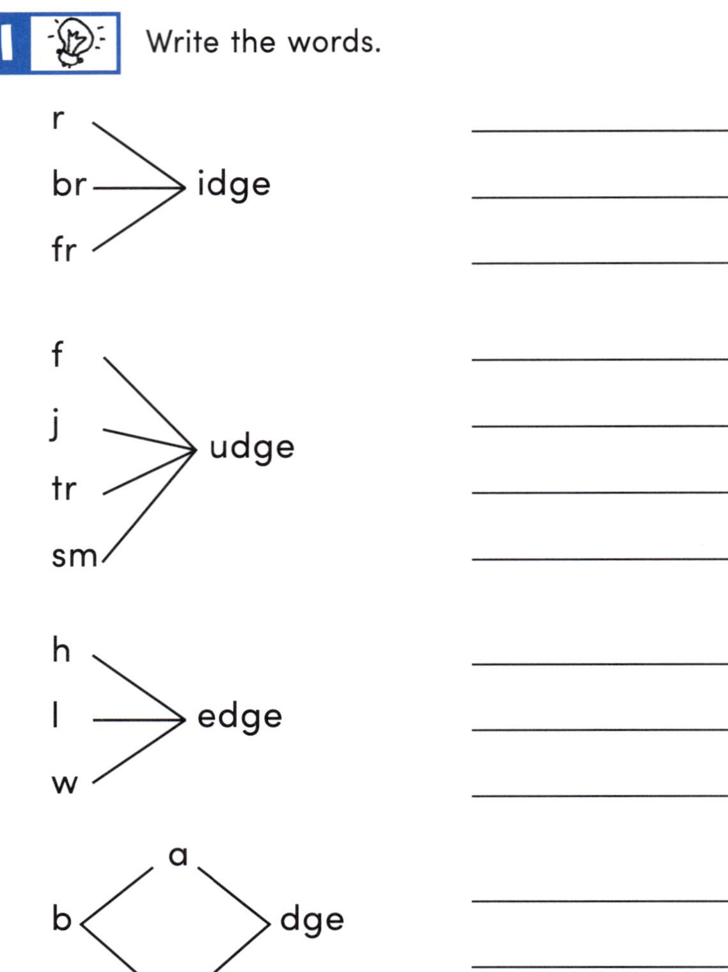

For words with the letter pattern **ge**, if a syllable has a long vowel sound, it is usually followed by **ge**. *stage* *large*

If a syllable has a short vowel sound, it is usually followed by **dge**. *edge* *ridge*

If there is a consonant before the end of the syllable, add **ge**. *change* not *chandge*

2 Write **ge** or **dge** to complete each word.

he ______	ba ______	fri ______	smu ______	hin ______
stran ______	mer ______	pa ______	do ______	indul ______

3 Use each clue to find a new word.

Rearrange *gifted* if you can't sit still. ____________

Rearrange *tagged* to get a useful device. ____________

Add **g** to *bride* to cross a river. ____________

Change one letter in *wedge* to make a living fence. ____________

Change one letter in *judge* for a sweet treat. ____________

Add one letter to *badge* to make an animal. ____________

Take a letter out of *fridge* to make a high strip of land. ____________

4 Proofread this text. The text has six words that are incorrect. Circle the mistakes. Then write the correct spelling of the words in the boxes.

The hamburger took so long to cook that I began to figget. Finally it was ready. Even though I ate carefully around the edge of the lardge burger, the tomato fell out and smardged my shirt. I quickly got a spunge and cleaned the spot. I had misjudjed my appetite and couldn't finish the burger so I put the leftovers in the frige.

5 Use the correct form of the verb to complete each sentence.

Uncle Jim is ____________ the pet show tomorrow. (judge)

The bored children are ____________ while they wait. (fidget)

We ____________ home after a long walk in the rain and discovered that Dad had made fudge! (trudge)

6 Write one sentence using both words.

badge
gadget

____

____

____

Reflection

- I can do this.
- I am not sure.
- I need help.

Unit 29

The Atlantic giant **squ**id has the biggest eyes of any creature. One squid had eyes 50 centimetres in diameter.

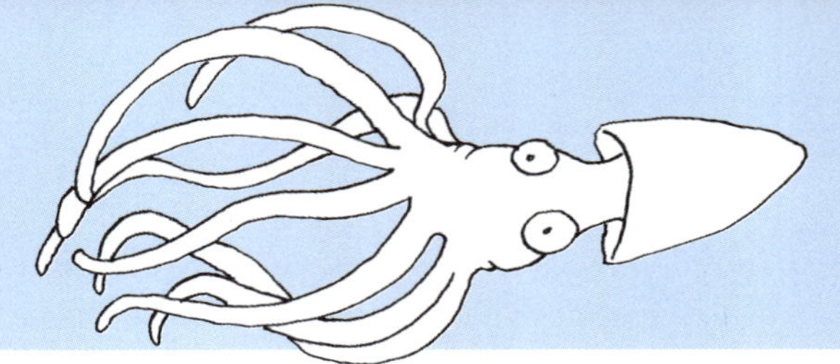

Say **L**isten **L**ook **U**nderstand **R**emember **P**ractise

quiet	____________
quite	____________
queue	____________
quarter	____________
s**qu**irm	____________
s**qu**eal	____________
s**qu**awk	____________
e**qu**al	____________
re**qu**est	____________
re**qu**ire	____________
s**qu**irrel	____________
mos**qu**ito	____________

Rule

qu is always followed by another vowel.
cw and **qw** don't go together in English.

1 Fill in the missing vowels to make list words.

sq _ _ r _   _ q _ _ l   q _ _ _ t

q _ _ t _   sq _ _ _ l   q _ _ rt _ r

q _ _ _ _   r _ q _ _ st

2 Fill in the missing letters. Match the word to its meaning.

_ qu _	a test
_ _ qu _ _	one of a kind
_ _ _ qu _	a jet of water
qu _ _ _ _ _ _ _	a colour
qu _ _	amount
_ qu _ _ _	fluid

3 Use your dictionary to find these words starting with s**qu**.

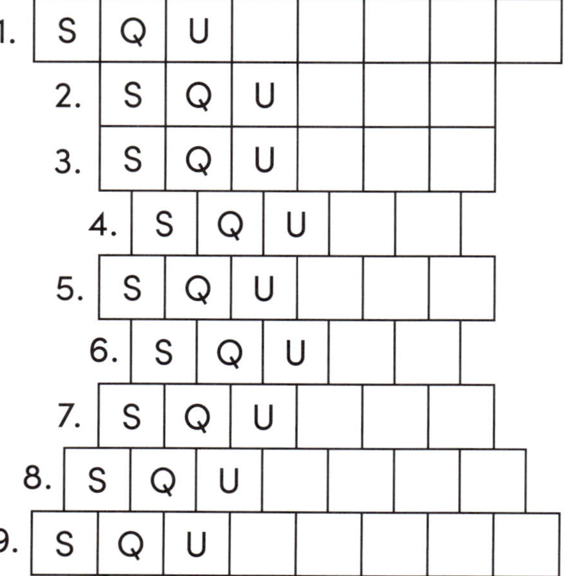

1. small furry animal
2. press together
3. look with eyes partly closed
4. sea animals with long tentacles
5. short high sound
6. crouch with a straight back
7. sound a parrot makes
8. shapes with four equal sides
9. line with twists or curves

Spelling Rules! Student Book 3 (ISBN 9780655092698) © Janelle Ho, Helen Pearson

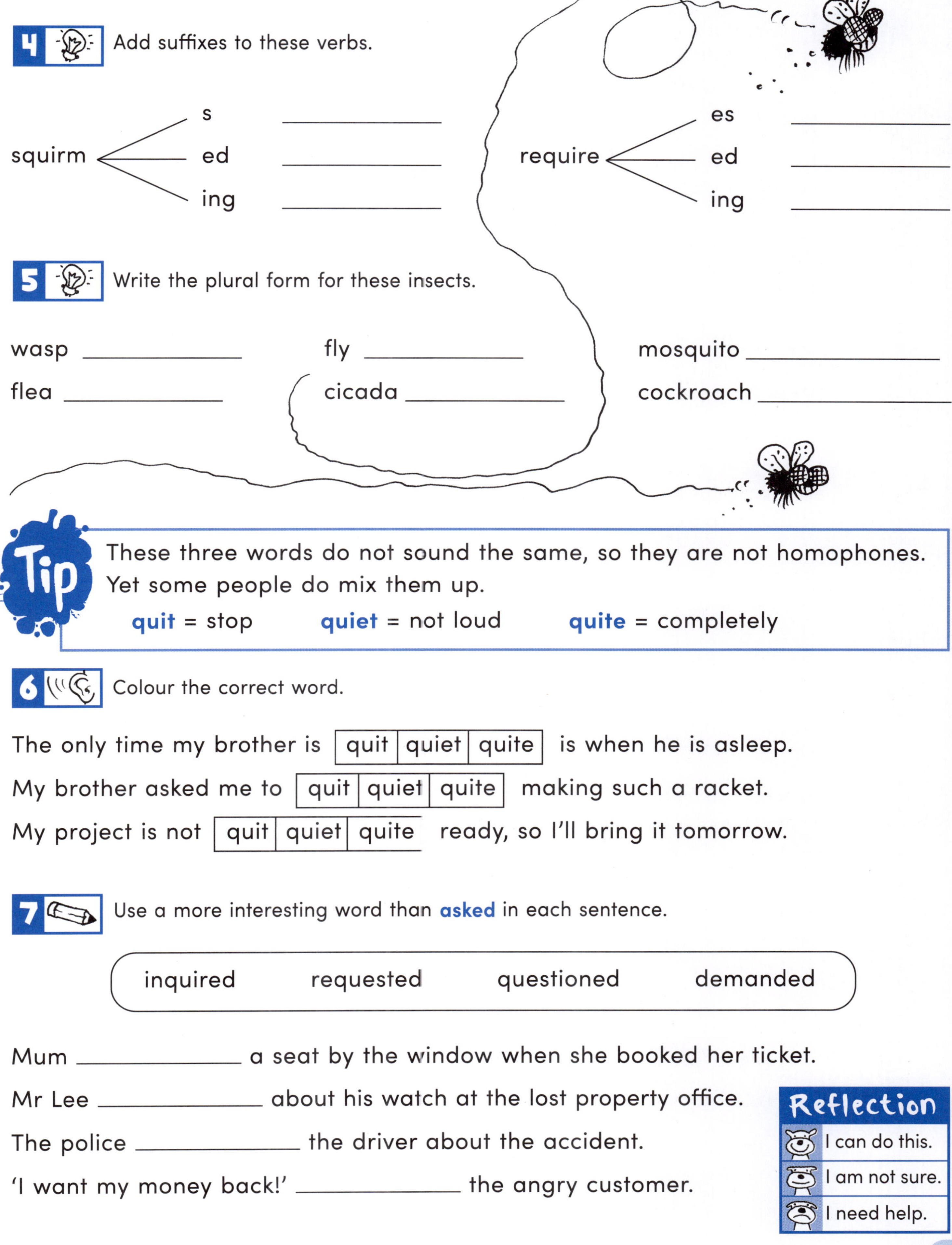

4 Add suffixes to these verbs.

squirm: s ______ ed ______ ing ______

require: es ______ ed ______ ing ______

5 Write the plural form for these insects.

wasp ______ fly ______ mosquito ______

flea ______ cicada ______ cockroach ______

Tip

These three words do not sound the same, so they are not homophones. Yet some people do mix them up.

quit = stop **quiet** = not loud **quite** = completely

6 Colour the correct word.

The only time my brother is | quit | quiet | quite | is when he is asleep.

My brother asked me to | quit | quiet | quite | making such a racket.

My project is not | quit | quiet | quite | ready, so I'll bring it tomorrow.

7 Use a more interesting word than **asked** in each sentence.

inquired requested questioned demanded

Mum ______ a seat by the window when she booked her ticket.

Mr Lee ______ about his watch at the lost property office.

The police ______ the driver about the accident.

'I want my money back!' ______ the angry customer.

Reflection

- I can do this.
- I am not sure.
- I need help.

In English, the **w**riting goes from left to right. In Arabic, the **w**riting goes from right to left. In Japanese, the **w**riting goes from top to bottom, in columns.

 Write the missing vowel sounds. The clues will help you.

c _ c _ mb _ r	long and green	m _ sq _ _ t _	biting insect
b _ c _ cl _	it's fun to ride	c _ l _ nd _ r	long, round container
d _ z _ n	twelve	_ q _ _ l	same amount
q _ _ rt _ r	four make a whole	r _ q _ _ st	polite question
q _ _ _ _	line up	g _ _ st	visitor to your home

 These words have lost their silent letters! Write them correctly.

thum ____________ casle ____________ iland ____________

gost ____________ nuckle ____________ nead ____________

autum ____________ rong ____________ onest ____________

tong ____________

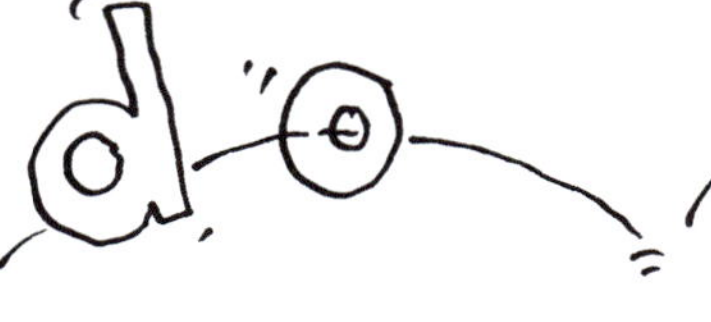

 Say each word aloud.
Draw a circle around the **c** or **g** if it makes a soft sound as in *cent* or *giraffe*.
Draw a square around the **c** or **g** if it makes a hard sound as in *cat* or *goat*.

correct	cancel	garbage	guilty
bicycle	gentle	century	garage
calendar	certain	grammar	cement

4 The missing letters all make a **j** sound. Fill in **g** or **j**.

_ uicy	_ ymnasium	_ iraffe	_ ewel
_ inger	_ olly	_ iant	_ enius
_ azz	_ igantic	_ ourney	_ enerally

Spelling Rules! Student Book 3 (ISBN 9780655092698) © Janelle Ho, Helen Pearson

5 Make word families by adding prefixes and/or suffixes to these base words. If you need help, look in a dictionary.

honest	__________	__________	__________
doubt	__________	__________	__________
decide	__________	__________	__________
quiet	__________	__________	__________
garden	__________	__________	__________

6 Complete each sentence using a word from the shape.

cents scents sense

Dad wants to buy some perfume. There are a few __________ to choose from. The smallest one is cheaper by a few __________. I __________ that Dad will buy that one!

we're were where

'Pack your bag quickly because __________ going away for the weekend!' Mum announced. This was news to me! __________ would we stay? What __________ we going to do? I guessed I would soon know.

7 Find anagrams for these words. If you have forgotten what an anagram is, see page 53.

plum __________

seam __________

sword __________

listen __________

asleep __________

cares __________

bruise __________

fluster __________

Unit 31

The world's smallest frog is from Cuba. It is just 8.5 **milli**metres long.

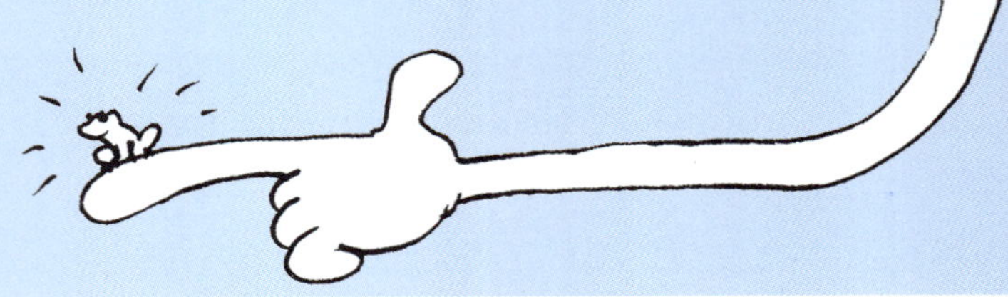

Say **L**isten **L**ook **U**nderstand **R**emember **P**ractise

metre ____________
kilometre ____________
centimetre ____________
millimetre ____________
litre ____________
gram ____________
decade ____________
uniform ____________
bicycle ____________
triangle ____________
dozen ____________
dollar ____________

1 Write the list word that is most appropriate for measuring each quantity.

weight of an orange ____________
distance between cities ____________
cost of a bus ride ____________
height of a person ____________
quantity of water ____________
length of a ruler ____________
length of an ant ____________
number of eggs ____________

Tip Some prefixes indicate quantity.

prefix	quantity	example
uni	1	unicycle
bi	2	biplane
tri	3	tricycle
quadr	4	quarter

prefix	quantity	example
oct	8	octagon
dec	10	decade
centi	100	centimetre
milli	1000	millimetre

2 Choose a word ending for each prefix.

pede form agon uple cycle opus imal angle

uni____________ bi____________ tri____________ quadr____________
oct____________ dec____________ oct____________ milli____________

3 Write the full word for these abbreviations and symbols. Then write the number of syllables in each word in the circle.

km	______	◯	cm	______	◯
mm	______	◯	L	______	◯
mL	______	◯	kg	______	◯
g	______	◯	$	______	◯

4 Write as many words as you can starting with each prefix. A dictionary will help.

uni 1	bi 2	tri 3

5 The letters of most of these words have been jumbled up. Write the sentences correctly.

I ma het olny mebmer of my faimly bron tihs cnetruy.

______

We hnug ornage rtinagles on eth fecnes to mrak het tarck.

______

6 An idiom is a saying that is used and understood by a group of people. Write the meaning of this idiom.

baker's dozen ______

______

Reflection

- I can do this.
- I am not sure.
- I need help.

Unit 32

The 'running man' **exit** sign was designed by Yukio Ota in 1979.

Say Listen Look Understand Remember Practise

exit ______
extra ______
expert ______
experience ______
extreme ______
example ______
exact ______
excuse ______
excellent ______
exclaim ______
excite ______
exercise ______

1 Say each list word. Sort them according to the number of syllables.

2 syllables	3 syllables	4 syllables
______	______	______
______	______	
______	______	
______		
______		
______		
______		
______		

2 **in** is a prefix that can mean 'not'. Add **in** to the words.

in + experience ______
in + active ______
in + valid ______
in + sane ______
in + exact ______
in + justice ______

3 Add suffixes to each word.

exit

+ s ______
+ ed ______
+ ing ______

extreme

+ ly ______

exact

+ ed ______
+ ly ______

excite

+ s ______
+ ed ______
+ ed + ly ______

Spelling Rules! Student Book 3 (ISBN 9780655092698) © Janelle Ho, Helen Pearson

Circle the word if **c** makes a soft sound as in *cent*.

exact excuse cyclone exclaim excite exercise

Why does **c** make a soft sound? ____________________

____

Write a list word for each clue.

way out

more than needed

one who knows a lot about a subject

cry out in surprise

physical activity

very good

something that happens to you

Instead of using *extremely + adjective*, use a word that says it all. One example is given. Use a thesaurus to find another. Then write with one of the words.

	Example	Your word	Sentence
extremely loud	noisy		
extremely big	gigantic		
extremely cold	frosty		
extremely quiet	calm		

7 What do you excel at?

____

____

____

____

Reflection

I can do this.

I am not sure.

I need help.

Unit 33

The first living creature to go on a space mission was Laika the dog, in 1957.

Say Listen Look Understand Remember Practise	
station	______
fiction	______
section	______
fraction	______
cushion	______
fashion	______
mission	______
expression	______
religion	______
million	______
champion	______
information	______

1 Write list words.

A millionaire has a ______ dollars.

I'll meet you at the train ______.

I am going to be a ______ swimmer.

One quarter is a ______.

I'd like to be an astronaut on a space ______ to Mars.

Bring a ______ to sit on.

Buddhism is a major ______ in Asia.

I can tell from her ______ that the orange is sour.

2 Would you look in the fiction or non-fiction section for these books?

A History of Our Nation *non-fiction section*

Life on a Space Station ______

Charlie Cheers the Champions ______

The Pyramids of Ancient Egypt ______

3 Write a list word to match each shape.

Spelling Rules! Student Book 3 (ISBN 9780655092698) © Janelle Ho, Helen Pearson

 There has been a word explosior. Find a noun to match each verb.

verb	noun
imagine	
explore	
infect	
prepare	
operate	
organise	
explain	
separate	

5 Find the **ion** words in the trophy and write them in the **suffix added** column. Write the verb that belongs to the same word family as the noun.

mountaincertainiron
suspicionmusician
curtainininformationjoin
maintaincontainexplosion
decisionaim

Base word (verb)	Suffix added

6 Write these fractions as words.

$\frac{1}{2}$ ____________________

$\frac{1}{4}$ ____________________

7 Use both rhyming words in one sentence.

fashion
passion

____

____

Reflection

I can do this.

I am not sure.

I need help.

Unit 34

The largest **pizza** ever baked measured 37.4 metres in diameter.

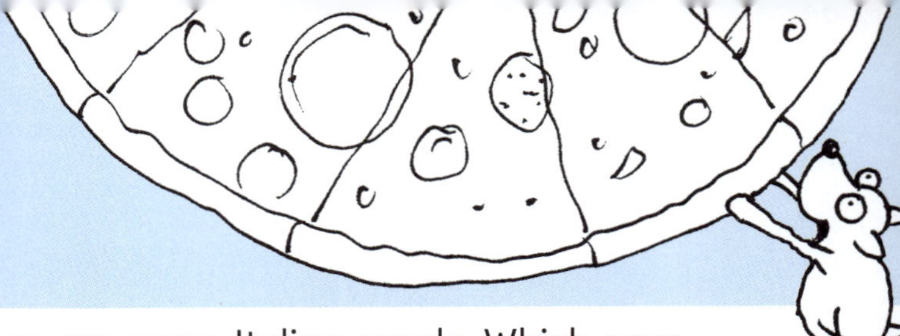

Say **L**isten **L**ook **U**nderstand **R**emember **P**ractise

igloo	______
robot	______
yacht	______
iceberg	______
khaki	______
tsunami	______
kindergarten	______
kowtow	______
pizza	______
spaghetti	______
chocolate	______
restaurant	______

1 Here are some Italian words. Which ones can you eat? Which ones can you drink?

cappuccino latte pizza spaghetti zucchini broccoli risotto gelato

Eat: ______

______

Drink: ______

______

2 Find a list word that fits each meaning. Write the word again.

_ _ _ o _ An Inuit (Eskimo) word meaning *house* ______

_ h _ k _ A Hindi (Indian) word meaning *dusty* ______

_ s _ _ a _ _ A Japanese word meaning *harbour wave* ______

_ i _ d _ _ g _ _ t _ _ A German word meaning *child's garden* ______

k _ _ _ _ _ A Chinese word meaning *bow deeply* ______

_ o _ _ _ A Czech word meaning *slave* ______

3 Write the correct word.

cacao cocoa chocolate

______ and ______ come from beans that grow on ______ trees.

Spelling Rules! Student Book 3 (ISBN 9780655092698) © Janelle Ho, Helen Pearson

4 Write the list word you might find in these locations.

The Antarctic Ocean ____________________

A factory handling dangerous chemicals ____________________

A large lake ____________________

A school ____________________

At a restaurant ____________________

The Arctic ____________________

Tip

Desert and **dessert** are often confused, even though they are not homophones.

desert = hot, dry place

dessert = sweet food

I'd like a second serve of dessert!

5 Colour the correct word.

It is often cold at night in the | desert | dessert |.

My favourite | desert | dessert | is jelly and ice-cream.

6 Colour the correct homophone.

We used a | course | coarse | sieve to remove the small pebbles.

Dad has just finished a training | course | coarse | for cricket umpires.

7 Write a paragraph about eating a meal in a restaurant.
Use these words: *restaurant, menu, course.*

____

____

____

____

____

____

____

Reflection

I can do this.

I am not sure.

I need help.

Some experts say the average adult speaks 12 500 words a day.

1 Complete the tables.

adjective	adverb
quiet	
extreme	
	funnily
	beautifully

noun	adjective
	dreamy
happiness	
honesty	
	doubtful

Holy adjectives...
It's the homophone!

2 Write the homophone for each word.

coarse	______	fore	______
hole	______	brake	______
peace	______	write	______
night	______	stair	______
steel	______	threw	______
blue	______	rap	______
new	______	guessed	______
fort	______	allowed	______
wait	______	eight	______

3 Homographs have the same spelling but more than one meaning. Give two meanings for each of these words.

cricket 1. ______________ 2. ______________

pupil 1. ______________ 2. ______________

coach 1. ______________ 2. ______________

match 1. ______________ 2. ______________

Spelling Rules! Student Book 3 (ISBN 9780655092698) © Janelle Ho, Helen Pearson

4 Use the clues to make a new word.

thought + 2 suffixes ____________________ excite + 2 suffixes ____________________

friend + 1 prefix + 1 suffix ____________________

obey + 1 prefix + 1 suffix ____________________

Write your own.

kind ____________________ ____________________

know ____________________ ____________________

5 Make a new word by adding a letter.

save	______________	(cut off beard)	piece	______________	(stick into)
hose	______________	(an animal)	word	______________	(Earth)
steam	______________	(small river)	truck	______________	(hit)
quit	______________	(bed cover)	treat	______________	(warning)

6 Change one letter to make a new word.

suction	______________	(a part)	worm	______________	(group of letters)
green	______________	(say hello)	sample	______________	(easy)
pedal	______________	(an award)	candle	______________	(hold it)
belief	______________	(end of worries)	fresh	______________	(meat)
project	______________	(look after)	carry	______________	(Indian spice)

7 Make a new word by removing a letter.

trough	______________	(not smooth)	grain	______________	(get more)
violent	______________	(colour)	learn	______________	(slant or bend)
craft	______________	(it floats)	barrow	______________	(goes with a bow)
brain	______________	(healthy food)	thread	______________	(trample)

List words in unit order

Unit 1
brave
shade
brake
table
awake
aeroplane
while
beside
spite
alive
advise
promise

Unit 2
close
alone
erode
suppose
approve
wardrobe
huge
pure
cube
refuse
accuse
conclude

Unit 3
shook
blood
choose
soothe
bleed
breath
breathe
threat
explain
throat
poach
cockroach

Unit 4
know
growl
below
allow
touch
grouchy
pounce
mountain
royal
money
trolley
layer

Unit 5
across
always
about
around
almost
already
ahead
asleep
above
another
along
altogether

Unit 7
school
ache
choir
echo
character
chorus
chameleon
stomach
monarch
anchor
chef
machine

Unit 8
country
state
northern
western
south
capital
territory
Australia
New South Wales
Victoria
Tasmania
Queensland

Unit 9
Mob
Elder
Aunty
Uncle
deadly
gammon
tucker
humpy
yakka
yidaki
boomerang
marngrook

Unit 10
grief
relief
fierce
niece
sieve
thieve
believe
friend
weird
receive
ceiling
foreign

Unit 11
untidy
unlikely
mischief
misplace
misbehave
mistake
disagree
disgrace
disgusting
dishonest
disobey
discover

Unit 13
helpful
awful
harmful
peaceful
colourful
grateful
beautiful
helpless
useless
carelessl
fearless
lifeless

Unit 14
taut
haul
fault
pause
sauce
sausage
audio
flaw
thaw
drawer
sprawl
awesome

Unit 15
gallop
collide
tunnel
channel
tennis
rubbish
common
lesson
borrow
quarrel
affect
effect

Unit 16
apple
saddle
puddle
riddle
cuddle
bubble
bottle
kettle
little
juggle
giggle
wriggle

Unit 17
January
February
March
April
May
June
July
August
September
October
November
December

Unit 19
midnight
frighten
neighbour
rough
enough
though
through
thought
caught
taught
daughter
naughty

Unit 20
laugh
toughen
graph
photograph
autograph
elephant
telephone
sphere
trophy

Spelling Rules! Student Book 3 (ISBN 9780655092698) © Janelle Ho, Helen Pearson

alphabet
phrase
physical

Unit 21
puff
cliff
staff
shelf
wolf
scarf
wharf
thief
knife
handkerchief
yourself
giraffe

Unit 22
hero
piano
zero
radio
toe
canoe
kangaroo
taboo
sofa
drama
idea
era

Unit 23
kindness
happiness
revision
television
direction
friendship
kingdom
freedom
forwards
backwards
childhood
neighbourhood

Unit 25
wrinkle
wrestle
knead
knowledge
gnaw
gnome
hour
honest
island
tongue
doubt
ghost

Unit 26
carpet
cancel
once
lettuce
advice
cucumber
cylinder
because
decide
scent
science
scissors

Unit 27
gather
guest
guide
together
germ
gentle
genius
giant
large
stage
gigantic
gypsy

Unit 28
edge
hedge
badge
fridge
bridge
judge
nudge
trudge
smudge
dodge
fidget
gadget

Unit 29
quiet
quite
queue
quarter
squirm
squeal
squawk
equal
request
require
squirrel
mosquito

Unit 31
metre
kilometre
centimetre
millimetre
litre
gram
decade
uniform
bicycle
triangle
dozen
dollar

Unit 32
exit
extra
expert
experience
extreme
example
exact
excuse
excellent
exclaim
excite
exercise

Unit 33
station
fiction
section
fraction
cushion
fashion
mission
expression
religion
million
champion
information

Unit 34
igloo
robot
yacht
iceberg
khaki
tsunami
kindergarten
kowtow
pizza
spaghetti
chocolate
restaurant

LIST WORDS IN ALPHABETICAL ORDER

about	Unit 5
above	Unit 5
accuse	Unit 2
ache	Unit 7
across	Unit 5
advice	Unit 26
advise	Unit 1
aeroplane	Unit 1
affect	Unit 15
ahead	Unit 5
alive	Unit 1
allow	Unit 4
almost	Unit 5
alone	Unit 2
along	Unit 5
alphabet	Unit 20
already	Unit 5
altogether	Unit 5
always	Unit 5
anchor	Unit 7
another	Unit 5
apple	Unit 16
April	Unit 17
approve	Unit 2
around	Unit 5
asleep	Unit 5
audio	Unit 14
August	Unit 17
Aunty	Unit 9
Australia	Unit 8
autograph	Unit 20
awake	Unit 1
awesome	Unit 14
awful	Unit 13
backwards	Unit 23
badge	Unit 28
beautiful	Unit 13
because	Unit 26
believe	Unit 10
below	Unit 4
beside	Unit 1
bicycle	Unit 31
bleed	Unit 3
blood	Unit 3
boomerang	Unit 9
borrow	Unit 15
bottle	Unit 16
brake	Unit 1
brave	Unit 1
breath	Unit 3
breathe	Unit 3
bridge	Unit 28
bubble	Unit 16
cancel	Unit 26
canoe	Unit 22
capital	Unit 8
careless	Unit 13
carpet	Unit 26
caught	Unit 19
ceiling	Unit 10
centimetre	Unit 31
chameleon	Unit 7
champion	Unit 33
channel	Unit 15
character	Unit 7
chef	Unit 7
childhood	Unit 23
chocolate	Unit 34
choir	Unit 7
choose	Unit 3
chorus	Unit 7
cliff	Unit 21
close	Unit 2
cockroach	Unit 3
collide	Unit 15
colourful	Unit 13
common	Unit 15
conclude	Unit 2
country	Unit 8
cube	Unit 2
cucumber	Unit 26
cuddle	Unit 16
cushion	Unit 33
cylinder	Unit 26
daughter	Unit 19
deadly	Unit 9
decade	Unit 31
December	Unit 17
decide	Unit 26
direction	Unit 23
disagree	Unit 11
discover	Unit 11
disgrace	Unit 11
disgusting	Unit 11
dishonest	Unit 11
disobey	Unit 11
dodge	Unit 28
dollar	Unit 31
doubt	Unit 25
dozen	Unit 31
drama	Unit 22
drawer	Unit 14
echo	Unit 7
edge	Unit 28
effect	Unit 15
Elder	Unit 9
elephant	Unit 20
enough	Unit 19
equal	Unit 29
era	Unit 22
erode	Unit 2
exact	Unit 32
example	Unit 32
excellent	Unit 32
excite	Unit 32
exclaim	Unit 32
excuse	Unit 32
exercise	Unit 32
exit	Unit 32
experience	Unit 32
expert	Unit 32
explain	Unit 3
expression	Unit 33
extra	Unit 32
extreme	Unit 32
fashion	Unit 33
fault	Unit 14
fearless	Unit 13
February	Unit 17
fiction	Unit 33
fidget	Unit 28
fierce	Unit 10
flaw	Unit 14
foreign	Unit 10
forwards	Unit 23
fraction	Unit 33
freedom	Unit 23
fridge	Unit 28
friend	Unit 10
friendship	Unit 23
frighten	Unit 19
gadget	Unit 28
gallop	Unit 15
gammon	Unit 9
gather	Unit 27
genius	Unit 27
gentle	Unit 27
germ	Unit 27
ghost	Unit 25
giant	Unit 27
gigantic	Unit 27
giggle	Unit 16
giraffe	Unit 21
gnaw	Unit 25
gnome	Unit 25
gram	Unit 31
graph	Unit 20
grateful	Unit 13
grief	Unit 10
grouchy	Unit 4
growl	Unit 4
guest	Unit 27
guide	Unit 27
gypsy	Unit 27
handkerchief	Unit 21
happiness	Unit 23
harmful	Unit 13
haul	Unit 14
hedge	Unit 28
helpful	Unit 13
helpless	Unit 13
hero	Unit 22
honest	Unit 25
hour	Unit 25
huge	Unit 2
humpy	Unit 9
iceberg	Unit 34
idea	Unit 22
igloo	Unit 34
information	Unit 33

Spelling Rules! Student Book 3 (ISBN 9780655092698) © Janelle Ho, Helen Pearson

SPELLING RULES AND TIPS

To make a plural

If a noun ends in **o**, the plural usually ends in **es**.

echo → *echoes*

If the word ends in two vowels, just add **s**.

kangaroo → *kangaroos* *radio* → *radios*

If a noun ends in **f** or **fe**, change the **f** or **fe** to **v** and add **es** to form the plural.

elf → *elves* *life* → *lives*

If a noun ends in **ff** or **ffe**, add **s** to form the plural.

cliff → *cliffs* *giraffe* → *giraffes*

Past tense

Most verbs show the past tense by adding **ed**.

discover → *discovered*

Some verbs have a different form in the past tense.

write → *wrote*

Adding ful and ness

If a word ends with a short **y**, change **y** to **i** before adding **ful**.

beauty → *beautiful*

If an adjective ends with a short **y**, change **y** to **i** before adding **ness**.

happy → *happiness*

When **c** is followed by **e**, **i** or **y**, it usually sounds like **s**.
When **g** is followed by **e**, **i** or **y**, it usually sounds like **j**.

Synonyms are words with similar meanings.

Small and *little* are synonyms.

Antonyms are words with the opposite meaning.

Full and *empty* are antonyms.

Antonyms can be formed using prefixes or suffixes.

kind ***un**kind* *harm**ful*** *harm**less***

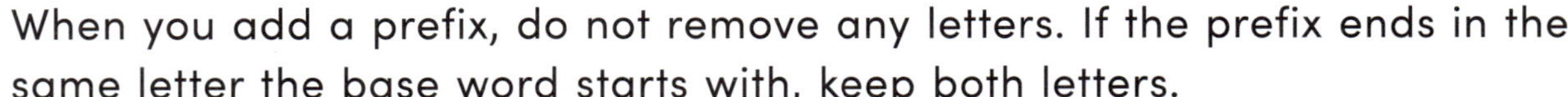

When you add a prefix, do not remove any letters. If the prefix ends in the same letter the base word starts with, keep both letters.

un + noticed → *unnoticed*

dis + similar → *dissimilar*

Use an **apostrophe** to show that someone owns something.

Tim's bag

Spelling Rules! Student Book 3 (ISBN 9780655092698) © Janelle Ho, Helen Pearson